The Mark of a Millionaire

Dexter Yager
and
Ron Ball

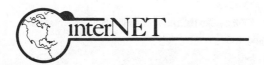

Published by Internet Services Corporation
Charlotte, NC

Library of Congress Catalog Card Number 90-71178

ISBN 0-8423-4043-2

Copyright 1992 by Dexter Yager and Ron Ball

Last printing 1992

Printed in the United States of America

00 99 98 97 96
16 15 14 13 12

The Mark
of a
Millionaire

To Nabra,

To my Lord and Savior,
who has given me the wisdom to live on,
regardless of what has happened,
and the strength to carry on
with peace, happiness, and joy in life.

THIS BOOK CAN CHANGE YOUR LIFE!

Often when reading a book, we fully decide to apply what we need to our lives. All too often though, weeks later, we have forgotten our good intentions. Here are 5 practical ways to turn good intentions into practical habits.

1. **READ THIS BOOK MORE THAN ONCE.**
    Let me encourage you to personalize and internalize these principals which have generated a turning point in the lives of many people by reading from cover-to-cover, then at least once again.

2. **UNDERLINE AND MAKE NOTES**
    Have a pen and a highlighter in your hand. Underline specific lines and paragraphs – a simple act that will triple your retention rate. Write your own thoughts in the margins and make it your book.

3. **RE-READ YOUR UNDERLINES**
    By underlining and highlighting, you can quickly review key items and portions of this book. Then re-read your key items over and over.

4. **APPLY THE MATERIAL IMMEDIATELY**
    There is an old saying, "Hear something … you forget it. See something … you remember it. Do something … you understand it."
    Apply what you learn as soon as you possibly can … it helps you understand and remember it.

5. **PRIORITIZE WHAT YOU WANT TO LEARN**
    Select 1-3 things from the book, apply them faithfully and make them a habit.

    Remember every person alive struggles with turning their good intentions into habits. Using these 5 points will turn wishing into doing and into habits.

    As I mentioned earlier, many successful people in the past have traced a new, exciting, profitable chapter in their lives to the reading of a specific book. I want that to happen to you!

Write the date you start reading this book: _____

May the date you have just written be the beginning of incredible blessings, rewards and growth!
                                                    — Dexter R. Yager

CONTENTS

PREFACE
CHARACTER
AND
SUCCESS

Recently I uncovered some material that I had not seen anywhere else. It comes from corporate research into why some executives rise to the heights of their company and why some don't. When I began to examine this, a lot of things that I've been talking and writing about started to come together in a new way.

I am enormously excited about what you're about to read. Maybe you have had just a taste of success. Perhaps that's enough to whet your appetite and develop your hunger. Or maybe you are too satisfied with it, and already you're slowing down and not quite punching forward to a new level of achievement.

What I want to share with you in this book are

the basic characteristics of successful people. I'll be making a lot of practical suggestions too--on how you can grow your business, expand your opportunities, and become more successful and secure financially. But what I have discovered is that a lot of those practical steps toward success happen naturally if you just work on developing the right kind of character.

When Bill Johnson, owner of the Ritz-Carlton Hotel group, began his business career, it was not with luxury hotels and it was certainly not as an owner. He got his start working for two men who had a new restaurant idea. The concept was a twenty-four-hour eating place named the Waffle House. Bill eventually was taken on as a partner himself. The Waffle House concept eventually grew into a much bigger enterprise—the prestigious Ritz-Carlton Hotels.

Later it was revealed why the first partners believed in Bill Johnson and why they made him a partner during the early years of Waffle House. They believed in his character. His integrity was solid. They knew he would add the skills he didn't yet have; the important thing was that he was a man of character.

It's really interesting when you look at the lives of the successful people in this world. Not just the Rockefellers and the Gettys and the Trumps, but the people around you who have become success-ful and wealthy. What you see is that these people have a lot in common. Their personality traits are similar, their behavior patterns are similar, their values are similar. These people have what it takes. They have the mark of a millionaire.

Dexter Yager

July 2, 1990

ONE
A MILLIONAIRE
DREAMS BIG DREAMS

I remember sitting in a hotel room in Belgium with Ron Ball a few years ago. He was telling me about all the goals that he and Amy he had reached in the last two years. He was clearly pleased with what hc had achieved.

But I detected a problem. I said, "Ron, you can't be satisfied with that. You've told me about goals you've reached, but you haven't told me about any goals you're going to reach. Let me tell you something that I have sensed in your life. I feel that you are beginning to stagnate and slow down. You need something to explode you in a new direction. I've got a challenge for you."

We discussed a few ideas—some new goals—for him to pursue. I remember watching his mouth drop open—it was something he really did not want to do. But I encouraged him. I told him he needed to do it, and do it now. Ron admitted that this was the challenge he needed, although it wasn't a challenge he *wanted.*

Ron made a few calls. He began to set up some meetings. Later he worked up a new plan. Two months later Ron reported that he was overflowing with new energy. He had new motivation and excitement. He had risen off a plateau and was achieving new things.

Ron had also learned about the first mark of a millionaire. A millionaire is a dreamer.

ALWAYS HAVE A DREAM IN FRONT OF YOU

We think of dreamers as being detached from real life with their heads in the clouds. But in fact dreaming big dreams is one thing that successful people have in common. Someone once said, "Dreams are the touchstones of our characters." A touchstone is a material that in old times was used to determine if precious metals like gold and silver were genuine. You slid the gold or silver across the touchstone, and if it left a mark, it was the real thing. In the same way, men and women with real, genuine character are those who leave a mark, those who dream big dreams.

Another way of talking about dreams is by using the word "goals." Goals are dreams with feet on them, dreams you can really get to. When you set a goal for yourself, you are saying this is a dream I'm going to make come true.

The problem you may be facing—even if you have experienced some success and have seen some dreams come true—is that you *stop* dreaming along the way. You find yourself sitting around without any goals in front of you.

Millionaires are always dreaming dreams, setting new goals.

But there's a deeper truth I want to share with you. When you set a material goal in front of you, that goal represents something beyond the material—it's not just the goal of a new ring, car, or house—*it represents the kind of person you need to be to have those things.* When you dream of a material thing, it really is a personal dream, and it says something about your character. You are really dreaming of the kind of person you can become: one who wants to give his wife a diamond ring, one who provides a better home for his family, one who creates a better working environment for his employees. You're dreaming personality dreams, dreams of who you can be, what you can be, and the kind of man or woman you want to be. That's what your dreams really are.

Now I know sometimes we get criticized for being materialistic. But God made the material world, and the material world is what we have to operate in. So material goals are an extension of who you are. Now, I'm not saying to eliminate the spiritual aspect of your life. In fact, later on, I'll be talking about that—how spiritual values are also the mark of a millionaire. I'm just telling you that your dreams—what you want—is good, because what you want is an extension of you becoming greater, becoming better. Sometimes you just need a basic material goal to spark you to a higher level of achievement and a higher exercise of power in your life. So you dream.

THE BASICS OF DREAMING

A dream gives you a future focus. A dream constantly pulls you, pulls you, pulls you to be better.

I was driving around the Lake Wylie, South Carolina, area recently. I pulled off to the side of an undeveloped piece of property. There was a bulldozer on the land, and some trees were knocked down. There was a lot of mud. It looked awful. It was ugly and unappealing.

It occurred to me as I viewed that property that even though it looked ugly to me, there was somebody somewhere who would look at that and say it was beautiful. You know why? Because that property is his dream. The way he sees it, the property looks the way he will make it look with his ideas and sweat and creativity. He probably goes there every day and works and plans and already knows what kind of a home he's going to build on that property. It's the focus of his future.

That story reminds me of the little rhyme:

> *Two men look out through the same bars:*
> *One sees the mud, and one the stars.*

Many times the dreams of your life are right around you. It's a matter of what you make of it.

A dream gives you energy. Many times—let's be realistic—you have to have energy, something flowing through you, to give you the power to get up in the morning. Because of the stroke I had a few years ago, I still have a lot of physical pain. Sometimes I will lie in bed in the morning, and I just don't want to get up. But then suddenly I'll begin to think about my dreams, my goals, what I want for the network, and the thousands of people who depend on me. Soon I'm not in bed anymore— I'm up ready to go. You know what I do every afternoon? I get up and walk next door to my log house by the lake—I've been building it for over a year, and it's not nearly finished yet. I walk over every afternoon and look at it, and it becomes fuel for me, because I walk through and see what I'm working for. My dream is fuel for my fight.

A dream is a fence against negative waste. Do you know that the term "mid-life crisis" did not exist eighteen years ago? If you examine the sociological and psychological literature going back to the beginning of the century, you discover that back then even the concept of mid-life crisis didn't exist. They didn't really have such a thing in their society. Now do you wonder, as I do, why that is?

Well, I have a theory about that. Today we have enough leisure time and so many career choices that it puts pressure on people. More and more, people can control what they will become, unlike the early part of the century when people were born into a social situation for life. Today, people wake up when they're in their thirties and they realize that they're not the person they really wanted to be. They panic, quickly reviewing all the various choices they still have in life. They wonder why they didn't accomplish more. They find themselves in mid-life crisis. But their real problem isn't making new choices—it has to do with dreams. Let me illustrate.

I knew a man who had accomplished some things in life, but never reached his potential. He was in his sixties. We were talking, and he was recalling parts of his life and expressing his dissatisfaction with himself. I asked him why he was disappointed in his life. He said, "Because I never learned to dream dreams. My dreams were there at one time and I just kind of let them go."

So many people today are facing mid-life crisis because they never learned to dream dreams. Their lives are sequences of events that happened to them rather than stories of dreams dreamed and fulfilled.

Listen, your dreams are a fence of protection against negative waste in your life. I'm talking about the waste of yourself—your talents, abilities, and your creativity. You don't have to go through mid-life crisis. If you have dreams, and if you believe your dreams can come true, you will wake up at fifty or sixty and realize not only how much you've accomplished, but how much you really still want to accomplish. Regret will never enter your mind—you won't have time for that because you'll be planning your next dream!

When Alexander Kroll was a young boy, he went out for football. He was so lightweight and physically undeveloped that he was wiped out the very first day of practice. He went home battered, bruised, and beaten. His mother told him, "Alex quit. You're too small—quit." He said, "No, Mom, I'm going to find a way because I'm dreaming of football—that's what I want to do." Alex had a job, and working a full schedule, he saved his money and bought a set of weights. In order to build his body up, Alex realized that the only time he could do it was beginning at 2:30 A.M. So he got up at 2:30 every morning, worked out, went to his job, went to school, came home, did his homework, and went to bed. He did that every day until he made the high school football team. But that was only one of his goals. He went to college and became a first team All-American. Then in his senior year he became captain of an undefeated football team. And today Alexander Kroll is the chairman and chief executive officer of Young & Rubcham, one of the most successful advertising organizations in the whole world. Somebody once asked Kroll in an interview, "What is the secret of your success?" Kroll replied—and I won't ever forget this—"I always have dreams that take my breath away."

Now, I don't know if you have dreams like that, but I want to challenge you to make goals that will take your breath away, goals that will shock you with their enormous possibility in your life, goals that will stretch you if you want to keep succeeding.

I can tell you this works from personal experience. In the late sixties and early seventies I began to dream about a networking business. I imagined coliseums packed with motivated people. I pictured thousands of cars streaming into our city just to be a part of our business. I organized a convention in Richmond, Virginia, as a start of my dream fulfillment. We had several hundred attend, but I still hungered for thousands. Now as the nineties have begun, the dream has arrived. We have so many tens of thousands in attendance at our Charlotte rallies that even the new 25,000-seat Charlotte Coliseum can't hold the crowds. We have to plan overflow locations at every site. And we are still growing.

It all started with a dream.

TWO
A MILLIONAIRE
CREATES A PLAN

Charlie Brown is at bat. STRIKE THREE. He has struck out again and slumps over to the bench. "Rats!" he says, "I'll never be a big-league player. I just don't have it! All my life I've dreamed of playing in the big leagues, but I know I'll never make it."

Lucy turns to console him. "Charlie Brown, you're thinking too far ahead. What you need to do is set yourself more immediate goals."

He looks up. "Immediate goals?"

Lucy says, "Yes. Start with this next inning when you go out to pitch. See if you can walk off of the mound without falling down!"

Well, I would think most of your sights would be set higher than Charlie Brown's, but this comic illustrates a very important point about dreaming: You must turn your dreams into targets.

Let me give you a simple, five-step method of doing this:

Write down your dreams. Now you may be thinking that this is a little silly. Maybe you think you can keep them in your head well enough. Why do you need to write them down? Let me tell you a story:

I know of a man in Atlanta who is very successful. Among his clients are Coca-Cola, Georgia Pacific, and General Electric. This man said, "We were taught in the beginning of our corporate training program that you do nothing without writing it down as a goal." That seems so simple and basic, but how many of you have specific written goals in every area of life for what you want? This is a vital element for success; you've got to do it.

Susan Bower owns a T-shirt and awards trophy company in Memphis, Tennessee. For four years in a row her company has been on the *Inc.*500 List of Fastest Growing Small Companies in America. She wrote, "The reason that I've been a success is that I take a notebook and every week I fill it with goals. I start crossing off those goals as I reach them." She never gets up in the morning without a list of specific targets.

Charles Stanley, the well-known pastor of the First Baptist Church of Atlanta, Georgia, tells how he and Anna, his wife, went to Stone Mountain, Georgia, in a camper. They stayed there for days and recorded every goal that they ever dreamed of, everything they hoped for, everything they wanted—they wrote it down and each one became a target. Dr. Stanley later claimed that those goals changed his direction at that point in his life.

Writing down your dreams makes them more practical, more immediate, and less abstract. The written list will remind you of goals you had set for yourself that you wouldn't otherwise be able to remember. The act of writing such a list becomes a commitment on your part that takes the dream beyond the pie-in-the-sky stage and puts it right on the table in front of you.

Divide each dream into smaller, achievable, immediate goals. Like Charlie Brown, many of us need to take our dream of playing in the big leagues and start to achieve it by simply learning how to walk off the pitcher's mound without tripping!

Let's take a hypothetical situation. Say your dream is to lose ten pounds. Start by writing that down on a piece of paper. Next, divide that dream into smaller goals. Perhaps that means losing two pounds a week for the next five weeks. So you really have five smaller goals—two pounds each week for five weeks.

Create an action plan. This means beside each of your smaller goals you need to write down the way that you will actively achieve your sub-goal. In our effort to lose ten pounds, the first week's plan may be to cut out all desserts. For the second week, we may decide to exercise three mornings. (Probably a better way in this case is to create a plan that includes diet and exercise and repeat that same plan five times, each of five weeks.)

Identify the kind of man or woman you need to be to accomplish your goal. Write this down as well. In our dream of losing ten pounds, we might write that we will need to be the kind of person who can control his appetite, and have the kind discipline to get out exercising several mornings a week. We might write down that we will need to have willpower to turn down the various snacks and desserts offered to us.

Finally, imagine yourself already having reached that goal. In my last book, I wrote about the power of visualization: "What exactly is visualization? It's a mental technique. You picture in vivid, clear terms what it is you really want. You create an intense picture of where you're going. You see yourself having accomplished your dream. That picture is constantly in front of you. You visualize it, you feel it, you touch it, you taste it, you see it, you live it."

This is one of the distinctive marks of a millionaire. You see, millionaires don't just dream big dreams. They imagine themselves as having achieved those dreams. This is an incredibly powerful motivational force, and it will unlock great things in you. When you imagine yourself ten pounds thinner, when you see yourself in that vice-presidency, when you visualize financial freedom for yourself and your family, then you will be activated to accomplish your goals and dreams.

Successful people not only dream dreams, but they turn them into a plan of action. And the simple, effective way to do this is to write everything you need to do to achieve your dreams.

You must develop a planning habit. It's a valuable technique. Have you heard the story of Charles Schwaab? A millionaire visited Schwaab one day. They were talking and Schwaab said he could give the man a system that would transform his managerial leadership. The millionaire said he would pay Schwaab a million dollars for the system. Charles said, "Sold." The next day, Schwaab walked in. He handed the man a piece of paper folded over. The millionaire opened it. It read:

1. Make a list.
2. Put priorities in order.
3. Do the list.

The guy crumpled up the paper and said, "A million dollars for that?" Schwaab said, "I told you I'd give you the greatest secret of management ever written." Well, the man wrote the million-dollar check.

The point is Schwaab was of the first people in the history of managerial journalism to ever come up with something so simple as just making a list. Up until that time, people thought that to make a plan you had to get a committee, discuss it to death, and take up a lot of time. Schwaab said no—just make a list, put priorities in order, and do the list.

Now don't you think if a successful millionaire paid that much money for it, that it should be quite valuable to you as well?

I encourage you to follow the four points I've

outlined in this chapter. Write down your dream. Write down smaller, achievable goals. Write down the person you need to be to achieve your goals. Then imagine—visualize—yourself having achieved the dream.

The movie *Lawrence of Arabia* is one of the greatest studies in leadership ever put on film. Remember, this film is based on the true story of T.E. Lawrence of England. In the movie there's one incredible moment when Lawrence is trying to convince an Arab tribe to go attack the city of Aqaba. He tells them that Aqaba can be taken because its guns are pointed to the sea: the Arabs could attack from land and their foes would never be able to halt their attack. The tribesmen said it would never work: you had to go across the desert; nobody had ever done it before. He asked them, "Do you want the Turks to continue to embarrass and savagely brutalize and kill your people?" They said, "Well, no, we'll fight. But we can't cross the desert." And they put up all their objections again.

Talk about a man who knew what he wanted!

A great dramatic moment in the movie occurs when Lawrence walks over to the two Arab chieftains, a father and a son, and he is utterly disgusted. He says to them, "We've got to try." The Arab son says, "What do you want from us? What should we do?" Lawrence replies, "Over there is Aqaba—we are going to go there." And he walks off. Now that's leadership. That guy knows what he wants. In simple terms he says, "That's what I want—Aqaba. Here's my plan. We're going there."

That story isn't just for the leaders of nations in this world. It's for you. That's the attitude you have to have in your family and business. You have to sit down with your spouse and write down how much money you want to be making in ten years: "Now, darling, we're going to go there. Here's how." You need to write down your dreams and goals and character requirements to make your business into a thriving success. "Partners, in five years that's where we're going to be. This is my plan."

It's that simple. If you follow through on this, you will have developed another mark of a millionaire, for you will have created a plan to fulfill your dreams.

THREE
A MILLIONAIRE
TAKES ACTION

In 1939 the United States of America was not prepared for international war. Global conflict was the farthest thing from the minds of most Americans. They knew there were threatening rumbles overseas that were beginning to stir up the European economic situation and political situation, but they wanted nothing to do with European conflict. Isolationism was the dominant philosophy of the day—meaning there were two gigantic oceans to protect America, and the prevailing thought was, "We'll stay on our side of the world and you stay on yours. You leave us alone and we'll leave you alone"—isolationism.

One man refused to swallow the drug of isolationism. Franklin Roosevelt knew that America must be mobilized because war would soon touch our own shores. He knew we had to do something to help England and other countries resist the terrible evil of Nazi Germany. So, Roosevelt secretly began to harness the energy of America to strengthen our military system. In 1939 our military was a joke. We had an almost nonexistent air force. Our army, our land-based military forces, were fourth- or fifth rated in the world. We were not at all respected in terms of military might or muscle. We couldn't handle ourselves in a straight-ahead fight with any other major nation. So Roosevelt began to pull together appropriations bills and resources from different sources. Gradually, behind the scenes, he began to strengthen the military. He knew the time would come when America would have to stand strong and fight the evil of Nazi Germany. As 1939 began to draw to a close, the world began to see the wisdom of Roosevelt's policies. They realized that here was a great leader who knew that in order for America to be successful, she had to be strong. We could not delude ourselves into thinking that we could make it just hiding behind two oceans.

What does this have to do with you and me? You are in a position right now where you can succeed or you can fail—the choice is entirely up to you. What it takes is action. Just as Schwaab said: "Make a list. Prioritize the list. Do the list." What you need to do is "do the list." Do your dream.

Roosevelt was willing to take action—actually a series of small, but significant actions—before the rest of the country was ready or willing to act. That is the mark of leadership. That is the mark of a millionaire. And that, my friend, may be the hardest mark of character for you to develop.

Many people can dream dreams. Some people can develop an action plan on paper. But few people can really bring themselves to *do* their dream.

MAKING CHOICES

Acting on something is the same as choosing to do something. A famous French philosopher once wrote: "Do you want to know how a man can finally become evil? It is because he made so many little choices, but each one led him in that direction."

You're a product of your choices. You need to realize you cannot hide from that any longer or pretend that the choice is not yours. You can't blame your parents, your boss, your teacher, or someone else. It's up to you. You will become the sum of the little choices in life.

I sometimes think there are two kinds of people in the world: those who let life happen to them, and those who live by making active, conscious choices about what they want in life.

Those who let life happen to them are content to live by circumstance, whatever events befall them. For these people, though, not acting (not choosing) is in itself a act (or choice), although a cowardly one. These people wind up living by the choices other people make.

Those who take control of life and *act* upon it are determining their own future and enacting their own dreams.

LIVING LIFE ON THE ATTACK

You need to learn to live life on the attack. Some of you immediately shrink back from that statement because you think you're supposed to be loving and never attack anyone. But I don't mean that you strangle other people emotionally, or walk on people just to get what you want. Not at all—that would be wrong. I'm talking about being aggressive, not leaning back and waiting for circumstance to somehow take care of all your needs.

I know of a man who is the head of an organization in Atlanta giving an alternative to abortion for young women. He's putting his money where his mouth is. He is in there getting his hands dirty, trying to help people do something about the terrible abortion sin in America. Here is a man being aggressive, living life on the attack. He doesn't sit in his comfortable church and say, "Oh, well, now God, I hope you'll do something about our abortion dilemma." No, he gets involved, active. That's living life aggressively.

I read of a young man recently who had been so intimidated by his cruel and abusive father that he finally forced a confrontation with his dad, knowing that his dad would be physically violent. The young man told his friends, "I'm going to confront him, talk to him because I can't bear living afraid anymore."

Aren't you tired of being scared all the time? Aren't you fed up with being intimidated? Don't you feel like you've had it up to here with being overwhelmed by the negative forces that oppose you? Haven't you just had it? Don't you want to be aggressive? The God of the universe wants to help you succeed in fulfilling his purposes, and succeed in doing his will. You don't have to take it—and I don't say this in any unkind way—you don't have to take a back seat to anybody. You can live life on the attack.

Years ago a young black child was growing up in Cleveland, in a home that he later described as "materially poor but spiritually rich."

One day a famous athlete, Charlie Paddock, came to his school to speak to the students. At the time Paddock was considered the fastest human being alive. He told the children, "Listen! What do you want to be? You name it and then believe that God will help you be it."

The boy went to his track coach and told him of his new dream. His coach told him, "It's great to have a dream, but to attain your dream you must build a ladder to it. Here is the ladder to your dreams. The first rung is determination! And the second rung is dedication! The third rung is discipline! And the fourth rung is attitude!"

The boy acted on his dream, applying each of the rungs of the ladder to the achievement of his goals.

Later that he went on to win four gold medals in the 1936 Berlin Olympics. He won the 100-meter dash and broke the Olympic and world records for the 200-meter. His broad jump record lasted for twenty-four years. His name? Jesse Owens.

FOUR
A MILLIONAIRE
WORKS HARD

A major corporate study of sixty-two dominating business leaders all over the world, from the Marriott Corporation to Apple Computer, reveals that not one of the leaders was a classic workaholic— that is a person who is grim and driven and joyless and controlled and enslaved by work he hates, but is compelled to do it anyway. Not one of these men and women were like that. Instead they were "workaphiles" which means "a lover of work"—they loved doing what they did.

When we think of a classic millionaire, we tend to think of a person in a huge mansion on acres of manicured lawn. We think of servants preparing him meals and cleaning the house and grounds and chauffering him around. And we tend to think that a millionaire doesn't have to work, that he just lounges around, sipping ice tea by the big swimming pool.

Well, I've got news for you. Millionaires may own nice homes and cars (and even drink iced tea once in awhile!), but they tend to be people who work, and work hard. They may have a servant or chef or housekeeper, but it's simply by employing such people that a millionaire can devote more time to his work and his dreams.

So if you're reading this thinking that your goal in life is to become wealthy so you don't have to work, then you've got it all wrong. You can't really be successful unless you enjoy the work you're in and desire to work at it diligently. If your motive is to get rich so you don't have to work, then you probably don't have what it takes to get rich in the first place.

Whatever level you live at, you need to learn to love what you do and love the people you work with. Even if you're a PPP (professional paper pusher!), you can learn to like paperwork by thinking about what your paperwork is going to do for people. And maybe you can even learn to love it. Do you see what I mean? You need to learn to love your work, to become not a workaholic but a workaphile.

The truth is that success comes from hard work. The formula for success is there are no other formulas. The shortcut to success is realizing there are no shortcuts. It is all a matter of having a dream, and then work, work, work. Every person who has ever built anything significant has done so with labor—with the fuel and the capital of hard work.

Have you ever read the story of J. Paul Getty? I've told this little tidbit about his life before: When Getty died, he was a billionaire—the wealthiest man in the world. You would think he of all people could relax by the pool sipping iced tea. But even as an older man J. Paul Getty worked hard. This was even after his fortune was made. He was committed to the principle of work.

Let me share with you a few perspectives on the subject of work that have helped me immensely in my own life:

Work seems harder when it's less enjoyable. Someone once said, "Work is not the curse, but drudgery is." A lot of people say how hard their work is. But they're working harder in their mind than in their body because they're not liking what they're doing. Work is often as enjoyable as you make it. Real achievers often have to do jobs that they don't like. But they find ways of motivating themselves anyway. They choose to make work rewarding and enjoyable, and so it becomes exactly that. When you have a real love for your job, time doesn't matter. In fact, time flies, and you begin to want to work longer hours. You put in sixty to eighty hours a week and don't think twice about it because you enjoy it and you know you're going to be a success at it.

Successful people see work as play. I've often said that you make a living working eight to five; you make a fortune working after five. When someone starts thinking in terms of an eight-to-five job, they've already made their first mistake—they see work as something they have to get over with, instead of as a tool for their future achievement and promotion. Executives in big corporations don't work forty hours a week—they work sixty, eighty hours a week. There's a reason that they're executives.

OK, some jobs are tedious. But that's one of the keys to success in your work. Some people play golf; some people play tennis; some people play work. The key is to convert your mind from seeing work as drudgery into seeing work as play. Look for the fun in it; if there isn't any—create some. Get your mind off what you don't like and concentrate on what you do like. If you start changing your thinking, you'll find out that instead of hating your job, you'll start loving it.

Work is a privilege. Try to imagine yourself incapacitated in some way. Picture yourself in a wheelchair. Visualize yourself unable to get a job. Then think about how precious work—any work—would be to you. Think about how important it is to your self-worth. Think about how great it would be to earn even a little bit of money. If you can put yourself in such a situation for a short few minutes, then you will realize what an incredible, extraordinary blessing work really is. We take for granted the ability to work, and because it's something most of us have to do, we begin to resent it. But if we would only consider the alternatives, we would come to appreciate the gift that work is, and even come to appreciate more the work we're currently employed to do.

Work is a financial asset. One definition of work is that it's the ability to transfer your labor into a financial or material reward that you can enjoy. A few years ago a book was published entitled *Sweat Equity,* and it talked about businesses being built by young men and women all over America who didn't have much money. But these young people had "sweat equity," which was the monetary value of their labor. It was a tangible financial asset, and more than one successful enterprise was built upon the value of it.

Let me say one last thing in this chapter. Anthony Robbins, in his book, *Unlimited Power,* suggests that there are only two kinds of pain in life when it comes to success and work: either the pain of discipline or the pain of regret. Which one do you think is worse—discipline or regret? On the scale of your life, discipline and action may weigh ounces, but regret weighs tons. The mark of a millionaire is the discipline to work hard. Success is hard work in disguise. Many people want success, but they don't want work, and that's their first mistake.

FIVE
A MILLIONAIRE
DOES THINGS RIGHT

If you look at the successful people around this country, one thing you notice is that most of them are concerned with doing things right. They have a focus on quality and precision and efficiency in their businesses. They value common sense approaches that accomplish their goals in the best possible way. They avoid anything that smacks of mediocrity. And they're always looking for ways to improve the quality of their products and services.

Let me tell you five things that will help you develop the success quality of doing things right.

First, eliminate the Einstein excuse. To do your job better, you have to get rid of the "Einstein excuse"—that's the excuse that says, "Hey, I'm no Einstein. I just can't do this." You have to get rid of the Einstein excuse because it's a sure-fire technique to achieve failure. When you use the Einstein excuse, you usually wind up doing some-

41

thing a different, easier way. It also usually turns out to be the wrong way, or a less effective way that will yield lower quality. The Einstein excuse leads you into shortcuts that will damage your product and service.

For example, let's say you are in the business of providing an alternate postal service to customers. This is a business that has really exploded in the past few years. You've established a pickup with the UPS people, but you're their first stop, which is at 7:30 in the morning. You immediately use the Einstein excuse: "I can't do this. I can't be in the business that early every morning. I'll wait for the afternoon pickup." Of course, just one afternoon pickup means a delay for your customers who have delivered packages late the previous day. It lowers the quality of your service and it will, in time, damage your business.

Second, master the essentials. I came across a fascinating corporate study recently. It researched why fast-rising executives, after they started their careers and looked like sure winners, suddenly stopped. It usually happens from between thirty-six to forty-five years of age. They just stop climbing. They may still hold a high position, they may still have a corporate parking space, they may still go through all the mechanics, but they stop in their upward progress. Why? The amazing answer to this can change your life. The reason these executives stopped was that at some point they ceased doing the essentials and replaced them with non-essentials. They got off the right track.

It's like when you were in school. Remember how you decided to study at night, and then you spend all your time sharpening pencils and preparing your study area and sorting your papers? But you never really got around to studying. You did all the things that looked good, but you didn't get around to doing the job itself. You majored on non-essentials.

The corporate leaders in this study stopped dead in their career because they were majoring on non-essentials. They needed to master the essentials.

What is an essential? It is that without which the goal cannot be reached. It's what you have to do to reach your goal. What is essential for you to accomplish your dream? What is essential to keep your wife from having to work, if she doesn't want to? What is essential to you getting a larger home?

John Scull of Apple Computer says it's like baking a cake. You have to have the eggs, the flour, and the milk. You don't have to have the raisins, the spice, and the rest of it. But to have cake, you've got to have the basic ingredients. So what are the essentials to reaching your dream? Are you doing the essentials? This major study found that for these successful men and women, their success had ground to a halt because they stopped doing the essentials and filled their corporate days with non-essential mechanics that filled up their time but didn't reach their objectives.

Third, minimize mediocrity. Would it surprise you if I said that people actually *choose* to be mediocre? Well, they do. Of course, they don't look at a list of poor, mediocre, and excellent things and choose the mediocre ones. But they do choose mediocrity in other ways:

1. People choose mediocrity because it is easier than excellence. Excellence takes time and perseverance. Mediocrity comes naturally.

2. People choose mediocrity because it is life at the level they were taught to expect. A lot of people don't expect anything beyond what they knew growing up; in many cases that was the status quo, the average level of life.

3. People choose mediocrity because deep within their hearts there is not fire, but fear. They are afraid of striving for excellence and failing. It's like the quarterback who throws a pass twenty yards in front of the wide receiver; he claims instead that he was aiming for the halfback coming out of the back field. Only he knows the truth--he aimed for the wide receiver and missed. People don't want to aim for excellence, because if they miss, it demonstrates failure. It's easier not to aim so high and hit a mediocre target.

4. People choose mediocrity because of personal laziness. They're too lazy to take the trouble and make the effort that excellence requires. I found out something recently that really surprised me. In the Bible, in the Book of Proverbs, there was a word for laziness, which in the King James Version is translated "sloth." When I used to read condemnations of slothfulness in the Bible, I just took it to mean laziness. A slothful person is in fact one

who is lazy but also a person who in his laziness lives life with a joyless spirit and a bitter resentment toward people who achieve. Does that sound like someone who has criticized you lately? That is the heart meaning of the word *laziness* in the Bible. No wonder God hates laziness and is against it. It is a joyless, barren opposition to achievement.

5. Many people choose mediocrity because of a twisted concept of humility. Sometimes people choose to be mediocre because they believe God is happier with someone who is humble, and they believe that to be truly humble you really shouldn't succeed quite so much. To these people there is great virtue in being poor, in enduring failure, in actually avoiding the appearances of success. Well that's not the God of the Bible. No, it's not. I believe it takes more humility to be successful and humble than to be mediocre and humble. I believe God wants us to reach our full potential. He wants us to achieve excellence.

So how to you minimize mediocrity? Let me give you a quick little program to do just that:

1. Find a reason not to be mediocre—a dream. We've already talked about that, but if you're still having a problem with mediocrity, you may need to go back and check to see if you really have the future focus of a dream. To be successful, you must really want something so bad that it becomes a part of you and motivates you urgently to achieve it.

2. Develop some pride in yourself. We tend to think that it's wrong to be proud. But there are two

kinds of pride in the Bible. There is a pride that God condemns—an ego-dominated arrogance that walks over people. That's the wrong kind of pride. But another, healthy kind of pride is self-respect. It is rooted in Bible verses like "Love your neighbor as you love yourself." You have to have some self-respect first before you can deal with other people with any kind of love.

3. Win the little battles. Don't be so overwhelmed by the requirements of excellence that you don't strive for it at all. Start achieving excellence in little ways. Pay your bills on time. Develop a reputation for honesty. Work on that difficult relationship. Make one part of your dream the best it can be.

So, dream, develop pride in yourself, and work on winning the little battles, and you'll be sure to avoid the mud of mediocrity.

Another way to do things right is to make no exceptions. Frank Pittman, a psychiatrist in Atlanta, tells how he stopped a bad habit. He had wanted to stop the habit for years. Here's what he did. For several years, every time he tried to quit, he failed. Pittman said, "You know why I failed? I failed because I always made exceptions. I would say, 'I will never do this again—unless I'm having a bad day.'" And so every two or three days he had a bad day. Finally, one day he realized that his only hope of reaching his goal was to say "No exceptions!" If you're willing to say "No exceptions," you'll attain your goal.

Look for a better way. One of the marks of a millionaire is the constant desire to improve and to do something better. Companies that have an initial success, but thereafter ride on their laurels and make no effort to improve, are companies that ultimately decline and die. People who achieve something but then just sit and enjoy the attention, are people who will settle at the level of mediocrity. Their products and services and personal quality will always be just a little less than what others want and expect.

Millionaires do things the right way. They eliminate excuses, master the essentials, minimize mediocrity, and look for ways to improve. Take a clue from them. In acting out your dream, do things right.

SIX
A MILLIONAIRE
OVERCOMES HIS FEARS

Right now you may be full of excitement, motivation, and power. You may have discovered your dream, made a plan, motivated yourself to act, committed yourself to work hard, and risen above mediocrity, but in the hidden recesses of your heart, you have hidden fears. You have private anxiety, private terror that haunts you. This is the number one reason most people fail in their lives and jobs and careers. Fear paralyzes people.

You need to get rid of it. And by eliminating those private fears from your life, you're going to get powerfully motivated. Not only will you be free of these fears that have plagued you, but this process is going to catapult you to a new level of success. It's going to release you to be more than you've ever dreamed you could be.

So, let's get started.

TYPES OF FEARS

First, I want you to focus on your own private fears. I've found that fear really comes in three categories: (1) pain—physical, emotional, psychological, spiritual, financial; (2) personal embarrassment and rejection; and (3) being out of control (which is why people fear aging and death). Private fears come under those three headings.

Now all three types of fear have an amazing effect on you physically and psychologically. They are like weights on your back. They are roadblocks to your success. Let me explain in a little more detail:

Fear produces stress. The American Medical Association has linked fear, anxiety, and worry with negative stress effects on your body. One way that fear stabs you in the back is you have stress that begins to drag you and pull you down and strangle you. Did you realize that the primary prescription drug in the United States is no longer Valium? It's something called Tagamet. It's for stomach problems. It's a stress and ulcer drug.

Fear produces depression. There is an amazing study out of southern California. A group of university students, as reported in the New England Journal of Medicine, determined that a positive mental attitude was responsible for better health and lower levels of depression on the part of these university students. The students had problems with depression until they learned the techniques of a positive mental attitude and approach toward life. Depression even lowers your white blood cell count. That means that if you're depressed frequently, it will have a gradual effect on your body's immune system; you'll become more susceptible to disease and to health problems. Depression is rooted in fear.

Fear makes you stop trying. Your fears become larger than life, they take on a power of their own and your fears stop you and challenge you and you think because of your fears you can't do something.

So what is the answer? You must learn how to create your own courage. I'm going to give you a battle plan for that. But let's take a look at courage first. Courage is not an absence of fear. Courage really only occurs in the presence of fear. It's an invisible quality that becomes visible when there's something to be afraid of. The Vietnam vet who nearly lost his life trying to save the life of his buddy in the jungles of Southeast Asia wouldn't say he felt no fear. He will say he was terrified—but something took over and compelled him to save his friend's life. You may be scared silly, but courage take sover and does the job anyway.

CREATING COURAGE

Now where does courage come from?

1. Courage is created by the passion of a higher cause in your life. When you believe that something is so important that you're willing to give your life, your guts, and your soul for it, it will begin to stir courage within you. Some of you are just beginning to get a glimpse of a higher call in

your life. You're just beginning to see what you can do for your children and family; you're getting a dream of what you can do for your family financially. And this becomes a higher cause.

2. The pull of tough commitments creates courage. When you learn to discipline yourself, and when you learn tough commitments, those commitments will begin to pull you up and away from your fears. Fear will try to suck you down, but your commitments—your responsibilities—become goals that motivate you. The commitments you make to your wife or husband will take on power and start creating courage.

3. Focusing on the sheer pleasure of real achievement creates courage. Courage can be created when you start to taste the power of success. This goes back to what I said about visualization. When you see yourself in the role of being successful, then you have the motivation—and the courage—to overcome your private fears.

A BATTLE PLAN TO OVERCOME FEAR

I believe the next six principles will work on any fear you've got. These six steps will show you how to overcome your fears and how to empower yourself to create your own courage, no matter what situation you're in:

Make friends with facts. In the book *The Renewal Factor* by Bob Waterman (he co-authored *In Search of Excellence* with Tom Peters, one of the best-known management consultants in the world), Waterman says you will never win and win big until you become friends with facts. He's saying that you need to face anything that's a fact and not fight it. If it's the truth, then learn to work with it, accept it, and do something about it. At first you may not like this because some facts are bad news. You don't want to hear them. But really, every fact is a friend of yours.

Listen to this—it can free you. Every fact is your friend because you can't do anything without accurate information. So, if you have facts in your life that you run away from—maybe you're a pathetic money manager or perhaps your wife is trying to say something to you and you just won't listen—pay attention. Is what you're running from a fact?

You see, you can't be successful until you build on the truth. People who avoid facts are people who build on falsehoods and illusions. Sometimes people can gain a measure of success that way, but it doesn't last long. It isn't a strong foundation. Empires have sunk into the sand because they've been built on falsehood and illusion. One look at the Soviet Union and Eastern Europe today testifies to this.

If you make facts into friends, then you'll learn something about your fears. When you face your fears, they begin to lose their power. Their power begins to fade.

Now, let's be honest. I know that some of you like your fears. You like all the attention you get, you like the sympathy you create, you like the response you get from other people.

I heard of a woman recently who had a bad foot and limped around for years. The doctors couldn't find anything wrong with this woman. She went to doctor after doctor, asking what was wrong with her foot. Nothing was ever found wrong with her foot. Finally she went to a professional counselor. He said to her, "There's nothing wrong with your foot, is there?" She said, "Well, no, there isn't anything physically wrong." He asked, "When you were a little girl, what happened?" She said, "I injured my foot, and everybody treated me so special." The counselor told her that she had learned a negative, unhealthy, neurotic pattern. She had duplicated it as an adult with her foot fallacy. The woman simply said to him, "You're right. You're totally right." After that her foot "healed"—nothing was wrong with it in the first place. But three months later she returned with the same limp. The counselor said he thought she had understood her problem, that there was no problem with her foot. And the woman said, "I know. But I went home, and nobody treated me special anymore."

What an emotionally crippled way to live. But, you know, in our own ways, many of us are just like that woman. We like our fears. They comfort us in strange, unhealthy ways.

You don't want your greatest joy in life to be sympathy from other people. You know what's better than sympathy? Respect is better, and you earn respect. So make friends with the facts. Listen, if your bank calls you and says your mortgage is three months late and they're going to come after your house, don't get mad at the bank and deny the facts. Realize what the facts are, and building on the facts, do something about the situation. So always look for the facts and realize that facts are your friends. Don't be afraid of them. That's the first step in creating your own courage.

Control your imagination. In the first thirty seconds of dealing with a fear, what you think about and how you think about it will release supporting emotions. Whenever you face a crisis, a challenge, a problem, or a fear, those initial thoughts—your imagination in those moments—will turn you toward something positive or negative. Don't ever forget this.

This is a way you can win. In the first thirty seconds of the fear, you're going to release either positive emotions or negative emotions—but *you* are the one who is going to release them. So the power of your imagination is awesome.

This principle needs an example. Suppose you are suffering from depression, and you come to see me, a counselor. If I'm from the traditional school, I would say, "Now, why don't you sit down and tell me why you are so depressed?" The problem with that is if you tell me why you are depressed, you'll probably get more depressed just by rehearsing what it is that is causing the depression. Now what should I do instead? I should say to you, "*How* are you depressed?" In other words, what triggers depression? You're probably not depressed twenty-four hours a day, seven days a week. What do you do to trigger it? How do you walk, what do you think about, what do you imagine? You see, you are doing something to put yourself in a depressed state of mind. Certainly the circumstances that befell you were really tough, but it's *how* you handle them—not *why* they happened— that is crucial.

While we're on the subject of depression, let me make one further point. You cannot feel depressed while you are acting confident. It's simple, and it's an amazing truth. Now, I told you that I want to give you accurate information, so let me tell you something that's really important. There are some serious forms of depression that are psychotic or biochemical in nature through some hormonal imbalance in your system. There are some kinds of depression that do need medical treatment. But here I'm talking about average, ordinary, "I feel sorry for myself" depression, times when you just get overwhelmed by your circumstances. Listen, if you allow depression to rule in your brain, in your mind, in your imagination, then it begins to affect your body. One way you can fight back is by changing the body language of depression. Act more confidently, walk with assurance, stand with authority, and you'll find your depression dissipates quickly.

My main point here is that your imagination is powerful enough to give you courage to face your fears. Often the secret is what you feed it. I noticed recently that the latest installment of one of the most popular motion picture series in history has just been released—*Friday the 13th, Part 7.* What if you had a steady diet of what Hollywood calls these slasher movies? What if you watched that kind of movie all the time, and then what if you decided to spend a few nights at home alone with nobody around? You see, you have fed your imagination. When you were a kid and went to all kinds of movies, you used to feel fear sometimes in certain situations. Do you realize that you were duplicating in your mind a lot of the scenes you saw in the movies? You can watch a crime movie and then walk down the street, and suddenly you will imagine all these horrible things happening to you and get scared. So the secret of controlling your imagination is what you feed it. The Bible says, "Whoever walks with the wise becomes wise, but a companion of fools shall be destroyed." And the Bible also says that you are what you think about—"As a man thinketh, so is he." So, control your imagination.

Decide everything. We're taught in our culture that things are out of control, that we cannot control our destiny, that our future is controlled by our genes, that we are molded by our experiences as children. What happens in our society is that we begin feeling powerless, helpless, and out of control—one of the aspects of fear that I mentioned earlier. If you're ever going to be a total success, you must learn the art of making decisions. You have to take responsibility for your life and you have to be accountable for your choices. You have to decide everything because life is like a river and you're a boat, and if you don't decide to steer the boat, you're just going to be mastered by the current—you'll go wherever the river wants you to go.

Let me give you a great example of this. Many of you have heard of Harland Sanders. He was a wonderful, kind-spirited gentleman. He was a humble, committed, successful Christian man. Many of you know the story of how when he was in his sixties he had this great fried chicken recipe and a highway was re-routed away from his small restaurant. It became what is now known as I-75, a major artery in the east of the country, and they bypassed his little restaurant, leaving him stranded away from the traffic. He had to do something or go out of business. Here he was, eligible for social security, with a secret recipe for great tasting, finger-licking good chicken. You know what he did? He decided to do something. He got in his car and traveled for a year, showing this recipe and a new business plan to investors across the country. He got turned down 1,009 times. Finally an investor in Arizona said, "Hey, I'm gong to give this a shot." And now you've got Kentucky Fried Chicken all over the world. Colonel Sanders decided to do something.

Here's what I want you to see. When you're dealing with your fears and creating your courage, you are the one who has to make the decisions. *You've* got to do it. Harland Sanders could have said, *Hey, the Department of Transportation in the state of Kentucky has made my decision for me.* But no, he wouldn't let them make his decision. He made his decision. Win or lose, succeed or fail, he lived by the power of his own decision to do something.

Live aggressively. Teddy Roosevelt, one of the greatest Americans in our history, went through a brutal time in his early twenties. He lost everything in one day. His wife died in his arms, she had just had a baby, the infant almost died, and then he got word an hour later that he should hurry to his home because his mother had just died. This was a man deeply committed to his family. He was a young man who had physical ailments all his early life. He was weak in his eyesight, weak in his body. He loved his family and now they were gone. His dad had died two years before that. And Teddy Roosevelt said to himself, *I will not lose. I am going to become a part of the fellowship of the doers, and I'm going to do something great with my life.* He made this decision in spite of losing the people closest to him. He formulated an action attack on life and he fought his fears. You know what you learn about fear? You're going to learn that all your fears are actually cowards, and they will run when you attack them. When you attack, your fears will run for cover because they're cowards. That's what Roosevelt learned.

Let go of worrying about the inevitable. Don't spend every day worrying about dying. One thing is sure in life—death. Don't waste your time. If you don't learn to release the inevitable things in life, you'll squirrel away your time and energy on something that is non-productive.

So many people make this mistake in their daily lives at home and at work. They encounter a setback—a bounced check, a damaged car, a broken arm—and they fret and stew about it endlessly. They worry about what they should have done instead. In the meantime they expend precious energy on something they can't do anything about. Opportunities for overcoming their setback are slipping away.

Don't waste yourself and your emotional health on worrying about the inevitable.

OVERCOMING FEAR OF FAILURE

He was a man in his twenties. During those years he drifted. When he turned thirty-one, he thought, *I've got to get myself going and do something.* So he formed a partnership and went into business. In one and a half years he went bankrupt and lost everything. Then he decided that since he was broke anyway, he should go into politics. In his first local election, he lost badly. Two years later, when he was thirty-four, he decided to go back into business. He went bankrupt again. A year later he thought things were getting better, and he fell in love with a beautiful woman. She died. So the next year, at age thirty-six, he had a nervous breakdown and was confined to his bed for months. He finally shook that off, and two years later he decided to run for another local election. He lost. He went into another business, and he made a little bit of money. Then at forty-three, he ran for Congress. He lost. At forty-six, he ran for Congress again. He lost again. At forty-eight, he ran for the Senate. He lost that election as well. When he was fifty-five years of age, he tried for the nomination of his party for Vice-President, and was defeated badly. At age fifty-eight, he ran for the Senate again. Once again he lost. Finally, at sixty years of age, Abraham Lincoln was elected to his first office—President of the United States. Do you know that Lincoln said to friends late in life that he had had a lifelong battle with fear and depression, but he wouldn't quit? He had a battle plan for winning. He overcame countless private fears and endless public rejections to attain the highest job in the country.

Do you want to overcome your fears and create your own courage? Then remember this, your fears will stop you unless you stop them first.

SEVEN
A MILLIONAIRE
UNDERSTANDS
HIS WEAKNESSES

The corporate study that I have been referring to also found that you can build only so far on your strengths—good personality, gift for organization, etc.—but then the only way you will jump to the next level of accomplishment is by overcoming weaknesses that hold you back. As Frederick Harmon puts it, "Survival is built on strengths. Success is built on overcoming weaknesses."

ADMITTING YOUR WEAKNESSES
Successful people are usually very well aware of what they do well and what they don't do well. In many cases this has come from painful experience, from someone telling them face-to-face, or from

disastrous business endeavors in the past. One way or another, these people seem to have learned their good points as well as their bad points.

The problem that many people have is that they get confused about this. They think of a personal weakness as being like a failure or a moral lapse. It isn't. Not necessarily. All people have weaknesses. No one is perfect. Admitting a personal weakness is not a matter of personal failure. Quite the opposite. Admitting a weakness is a strong test of character. It is simply being honest and practical: "Such and such a thing is not something I do well." Say it, let go of it, and then work on that area or avoid doing it in the future.

In many ways this is similar to what we were talking about when we said, "Make facts your friends." You need to make the facts *about yourself* your friends. You need to be honest with yourself about your shortcomings. Then you need to build on what you do well and overcome those areas in which you are weak.

RED, YELLOW, GREEN

I've heard of one business consulting firm that follows a formula of identifying employees' strengths and weaknesses and breaking them down into three areas. Red represents those skills and abilities in which an employee is very weak. Yellow is the caution category—skills that show some ability, but can at times be weak. Green represents those things an employee does extremely well. The central concept of this theory is that an employee will be happiest if he or she is working in areas that maximize green skills and minimize red skills. The beauty of this is that it doesn't lay a guilt trip on anyone. The only problem a person has with personal weaknesses is when he or she fails to admit they exist.

I think that many successful people know this principle intuitively. They seem to have the knack of doing their high skill level areas themselves and delegating their weak skill level areas to other people who are better at those things.

COMMON WEAKNESSES

Of course, I can't begin to identify for you your personal weaknesses. But I do think there are some common weaknesses, shared by many people, that are patterns that hold people back every day.

The weakness of rollercoaster promises. That means that one day you're up and you promise people you'll do everything under the sun, but the next day you're down, and you break all of your promises. You're controlled by emotion and not decision, feelings and not commitment. So what are you? You're a roller coaster of promises. The way this works against you, of course, is that no one really can trust you. They may like you and want to believe you, but they're never really sure whether you will deliver. This is not just a personal weakness—it's also characteristic of many businesses and corporations. One way or the other, it's a definite character flaw.

The weakness of sloppy work habits. Ron Ball told me a true story recently. He sold his car to a business associate. He received the money for the car, but closed the sale almost two months later. The delay in closing the sale was because he lost the car title. Ron humorously related how he in desperation went out on the front porch of his house and prayed to God, confessing his sloppy habits that were the reason he couldn't find the title to the car. Right then a thought popped into his head: *Look under your daughter's old clothes and toys in the bottom of the third chest drawer.* Ron walked upstairs, opened the door, and picked up Allison's old play clothes. There lay the title. The point is that his sloppy record keeping and personal filing had gotten him into trouble. Sloppy work habits will sink the ship of your success eventually. Sure, if you're good enough and you're good with people, you can cover up this weakness for a while. But your sloppiness will come back to haunt you at some point.

The weakness of dishonest listening. That means you listen to people, but you never really hear them. Sometimes you talk too much and don't listen enough. Sometimes people come to you and want to tell you something. But you're so wrapped up in your own interests that you don't hear it. J.W. Marriott, Jr., of the hotel chain, said his whole life changed fourteen years ago when he was elected a leader in his religious organization. He had 750 people under him—school teachers, store clerks, housewives, and children coming to see him in his office. All they wanted to do was to be listened to. One of the great ways you can build people up is just to listen to them and to hear what they say. What's dishonest listening? It's listening and pretending to hear when you really aren't, when you're just waiting for an opening so you can put in your two cents' worth.

The fourth business killer is debt laziness. Now if you've read my other books, you know how I feel about debt. You need to get out of it. But given that you have some debt, nothing destroys a business reputation faster than not handling your bills on time. If you can't pay your bills, at least call and discuss it with your creditors. Work out a payment plan. Above all, don't risk your valuable business reputation by personal laziness in paying bills. That's a serious weakness to overcome.

EIGHT
A MILLIONAIRE
MANAGES STRESS

I've been writing to you about the marks of a millionaire. I've been telling you about the characteristics of successful people. But I'm not going to suggest to you that millionaires and other successful people never experience stress. Of course they do, and many of them experience more stress because of the power and influence of their positions. But the thing that sets them apart is that they have learned how to manage stress effectively in their lives.

We're living in the latter third of the twentieth century, in a time of enormous change, and some of you feel the pressure of that change continually. There are constant changes in your work. You need to develop new skills constantly. There are pressures at home. There are stresses in your marriage that continue to create friction and special problems. So, you are facing different kinds of stress, experiencing its damaging effects, and you need to know how to handle it.

A DEFINITION

The best definition of stress I've ever heard is by Dr. Hans Selye, formerly of the University of Montreal. He is now deceased but was a pioneer medical doctor in researching stress and its effects on the human body. Dr. Selye has defined stress in simple terms: "The wear and tear of daily life." Now I want to add to that Ron Ball's definition of the effects of stress: "The drain of your inner support system." You have a certain amount of emotional, psychological, and spiritual strength within you, and if you have stress continually over a long stretch, then your inner resources will begin to be drained of their power and energy. That can have a serious effect in your life.

Dr. Selye has given a list of thirty-four results of the effects of stress in your life and I want to give you this entire list, not to overwhelm you, but I want to give you the amazing effects of stress on the human body. It's incredible and you're going to think: "Wow, does stress do all that?" Now you may be feeling different degrees of stress right now, and some of these things will hit you and some will not, but these are all effects of stress.

1. Irritability
2. Hyper-excitement

3. Depression
4. Heart pounding
5. Dryness of throat and mouth
6. Impulsive behavior that is emotionally un-stable.
7. An overpowering urge to cry or run and hide.
8. Feelings of unreality, weakness, dizziness.
9. Abnormal fatigue—feeling tired when you ought not to.
10. Mental illness, emotional imbalance.
11. Floating anxiety.
12. A loss of the simple love of life.
13. Tension and alertness.
14. Nervous ticks and trembling.
15. You find you are easily startled by small sounds.
16. High-pitched nervous laughter.
17. Stuttering and speech difficulties.
18. Grinding of the teeth, technically known as bruxism.
19. Insomnia.
20. Nervous movement—you can't physically relax.
21. Frequent sweating for no reason.
22. A frequent need for urination.
23. Diarrhea, indigestion.
24. Migraine headaches.
25. Premenstrual tensions, or even missed menstrual periods.
26. Chronic lower back and neck pain.
27. A loss of or excessive appetite.

28. Increased smoking and cigarette use.
29. Increased use of prescription drugs.
30. Increased use of alcohol.
31. Increased use of illegal drugs.
32. Nightmares.
33. Accident proneness.
34. Neurotic behavior

So, do you see what stress can do to you? It's incredible. Everything from sleeplessness to nightmares and mental imbalance. Stress can have such a damaging effect on the human system.

George Marshall was one of the great military political leaders around the middle of this century. You probably know him by the plan to save Europe after World War II—the Marshall Plan—to pump billions of dollars into war-torn Europe, to rebuild that part of the world after a terrible war. General George Marshall had lived under stressful conditions for so long that when he finally came to his last job in government, as Secretary of Defense, he could not quite handle it. Friends of his said, "He had always been so great and so tough and so strong, something was happening. He was beginning to fade out and to escape." His closest friends knew the truth—long-term stress had begun to damage this great political giant. Here was a man of great ability, strength, discipline, and character, and stress began to have a damaging effect on him as well.

POSITIVE AND NEGATIVE STRESS

Some stress is good for you. God will sometimes allow a pressure situation to erupt in your life and knock you off dead center. Sometimes, if you're a Christian (perhaps you are not, and I respect that—but I have to make that clear when I share something like this because I believe Jesus Christ alone is the true secret of handling all the pressures of life), God will allow an almost inexplicable situation of stress in your life to get your attention and get you to realize he has something for you and he wants you to change directions. So sometimes stress can be positive.

But most stress is negative and has negative effects on you. Many of you are familiar with the "trauma list" that was compiled a few years ago. It rates the effects of stress in your life. It identifies a number of common things that could happen to you in your life, and it assigns them a point value relating to the level of stress that event creates in a person. The higher number of points, the greater the level of stress.

The first event is the death of a spouse, and it creates a great amount of stress in a person's life. It receives 100 points. Divorce follows second, which is really very close to the death of a spouse, but it's rated at just below 100 points. I noticed one item listed as the "gaining of a large sum of money" and right next to it was another item identified as "losing a large sum of money." Here's what I want you to see. If you gain a large sum of money unexpectedly, or if you lose a large sum of money unexpectedly, according to this study, the stress effects on you are almost equal. Now you say, "You mean to tell me that I feel the same amount of stress if I gain money as if I lose money?" Well, I'll admit that it is better to get the money, and you can do some things with the money that can help alleviate your stress, but the point is that getting a large sum or losing a large sum is almost identical in the stress that it creates in your life. So, here is an example of positive stress and negative stress, but they both create problems.

INTERNAL AND EXTERNAL STRESSES

According to most medical professionals, those things that create stress for you are called stressors. They can be two kinds: internal or external. External stressors can be a phone call at 10:00 P.M. from a collection agency demanding, "You have got to pay this bill." You think they're after you. What are you going to do? That's an external stress.

What about internal stress? Do you realize you can create stress inside yourself? You can make situations worse than they really are. Picture a situation where a man calls you and says he needs to discuss something with you, and then he arranges a time to talk with you later that night. But between the first conversation and the second you worry and imagine everything conceivable that could go wrong. When the second conversation occurs, you find that imagining all those terrible things was much worse than the actual problem. Now, the problem needed attention, and may have even been serious. But attacking the problem and meeting the challenge was a lot easier than wallowing in worry and imagining those six things that could go wrong. Your imagination became your enemy at that point because you fed it negatively and it responded negatively. So you can be your own worst enemy when it comes to stress. You can create internal stressors in your life.

It can work the other way—when you underestimate the severity of a situation. Let me give you an example. Suppose there's a new task in your job situation. For some reason you are expecting things to be easy. You get into the task, and it takes more work than you anticipated. Along with it come more pressure and tension. Your low expectations aggravated the stress of the situation.

This is also true by the way you talk about a situation. Sometimes your talk is so negative that you create more stress. You see, you can *stretch* your *stress.* If you were to just deal with the problem decisively and try to handle it, that's one thing. But if you continually talk about it negatively, you take your stress and pull it and stretch it out and make your stress that much worse. Wake up! Don't stress yourself out.

SMTS—STRESS MANAGEMENT TECHNIQUES
By the creative and mature use of the following stress management techniques, you can help

yourself manage the effects of stress in your life.

1. Physical exercise. Some of you may need to check with your doctor on this, and I understand that. But you see, God made you a whole person—not just mind, not just body, and not just spirit—but a whole person. What affects one part of you will affect the rest of you. So, you need to exercise to help you cope with stress. A brisk walk is great exercise and will help you think more clearly.

2. A new hobby. The problem many people have is that they have no leisure time activities that take their minds off of their work and their stresses. Develop a new hobby, or renew an old one, and you'll find this to be a good way of coping with stress.

3. Improve your eating habits. If you are overeating or undereating in reaction to stress, or if your indigestion is beginning to bother you, then remember that you can help yourself by just starting to eat sensibly. A balanced diet is so important. The problem is that when stress makes life more hectic, our eating habits are often the first thing we sacrifice.

4. Get more sleep. There is a very real, very serious problem known as sleep deprivation, and if it goes on for long, it can affect your decision making, your emotions, and your personal stability. So, maybe you need to sleep more.

5. Take a vacation. Now, taking time off or vacationing will not do you one bit of good if you carry the problems with you and you don't get away from them. If you lie on a beach and stew over everything, then you might as well not even waste your money on the trip.

Some of you may feel terribly guilty for taking time off. I came across a great quote from a motivational business speaker named Tom Hopkins. He said you should do the most productive thing possible at every moment. But then he explained what he meant—that sometimes the most productive thing you can do is nothing. Sometimes you need to un-string yourself and relax the tension before you will be able to handle your situation properly. If you find you're getting a lot of mental blocks in your work, and you can't think clearly in coming up with solutions for your problems, then you may need to just lay off, to take time off. That's not laziness. Sometimes it is truly the most productive thing you can do. I often take time off by driving around late at night, thinking, praying, and looking at property. This helps me relax.

6. *Change your routine in some way.* Vary your daily routine. Brush your teeth differently. Take a bath instead of a shower. Do something different in your life.

7. *Involvement with friends.* You need other people to bounce off of. You need some trusted people you can speak with. You need a close friend you can confide in. So often, as people attain more and more success, they tend to isolate themselves from others. This is the time when they need to reach out to others and open up to friends.

WHEN COPING BECOMES KILLING

We've just looked at some ways that people can cope with the effects of stress. But there are some coping techniques that are unhealthy and extreme.

For example—alcohol and drug abuse. Now it's OK to exercise and take time off and vacation, those are normal stress management techniques. But when you start turning to alcohol and drugs to handle your stress, then your coping becomes killing.

There was a well-known motion picture out a few years ago with Burt Reynolds and some other actors and actresses. It was a popular film. There was this one point where Burt Reynolds was in a shopping mall, and he was trying to persuade his woman to still have a romance with him. They had broken up and he's distressed, and suddenly he just goes berserk. He gets entirely stressed out. He collapses on the floor of this mall, gasping for breath, and he looks as if he's having a heart attack. A large crowd of people gather around him and try to help, and a medical doctor who was in the mall with Reynolds, a friend of his, sees what is happening, runs up, and begins to help his friend. Finally, the medical doctor says to the large crowd of people, "Does anybody have a Valium?" at which point—one of the truly humorous points in the film—dozens of people open purses and search their pockets and pull out Valium tablets—everyone's got it. That's funny in that context, but it's a sad commentary.

If you're becoming chemically dependent, you're in trouble. Alcohol dependency and drug abuse—chemical crutches—are only temporary solutions. You may feel you need a drug to help you short-term, but it doesn't solve your problem, and it doesn't help you in the long-term.

The National Drug Treatment Service Center, which works primarily with business executives in this country, says that on a national scale, 75 percent of workers in this country admit using drugs while on the job. These are day workers, factory workers, business executives, upper management. And eighty-three percent of them admit to having used cocaine at some point. That's scary.

A second dangerous way to try to handle stress is through manipulation of other people. By this I mean lying, cheating, and tricking people for your own ends. I encountered a man once who admitted that he was empty and broken in his middle forties after having built a very successful corporate career. He said he had no friends left, and nobody trusted him. It was because he had walked on so many people. Even his marriage had been destroyed. He said, "I've lived my whole life as a manipulator, using other people. I used my wife. I used my children. I used my co-workers. I used every strategy I could come up with in order to get ahead, and now I'm a broken, empty, miserable man." He still has many of the trappings of success—the cars, the house, the money, and the perks, but he doesn't have peace. Perks without peace was his price.

Someone once said, "Be nice to people on your way up because you'll need them on the way down."

Sexual cheating—that's another form of killer coping. I wish to God this weren't true, but some people destroy their marriages, deeply hurt their spouses, and devastate their children because they have sexual escapades. I call them sexual escapades because it is an escapade to *escape* stress. And men especially, traditionally, tend to associate sexual power with power in other areas of life. Sexuality, virility, and sexual potency are associated in their minds with power, aggressiveness, and authority. Men are usually thought of as the aggressive one sexually, although that is not always true nor does it always have to be true. But the point is many people are cheating sexually, and that this is used as a coping mechanism for stress.

Another way that some people cope with stress in a damaging way is what I call job slavery. When you marry yourself to your job, you can destroy a family really fast. I know this seems to go against what I was saying about the mark of a millionaire being that he works hard. But job slavery isn't the same as working hard. It is working obsessively. It is possible for someone to spend ten or twelve hours a day working in his or her business, and to still come home and spend time with family. But a person who is a slave to his or her job is one who works obsessively in order to avoid other responsibilities. It may also be a way of compensating for financial slavery—the debts that have piled up and the problem of living beyond your means. The need for more income can drive people to unhealthy work patterns.

Let me mention another killer coping mechanism that many of you may not want to hear. I'm afraid it's prevalent in our society today, and yet too few people say much about it. It's what psychologists call passive escapism. I encountered a man once who said, "I'm thirty-two and I'm a successful attorney. I've worked hard and done well. I'm a partner in my firm, I'm proud of my accomplishments, but I've noticed lately that I'm trying to escape all the time. I've already given my wife away, she's divorced me. Now, all I do is stay at the office as late as I can. I come home every night late and all I do seven nights a week is watch rental video movies on my VCR. I rent movies by the dozens. I have no relationships, no friendships. It's work and VCR, work and VCR. I'm just submerged in those movies." That is passive escapism. It's passive because all you have to do is reach up, push the button, and watch it.

Now I enjoy some motion pictures. I am entertained by going to a movie, just like anyone else is. And sometimes I learn things from movies. But I were to go to movies all the time, to become a "movie-holic," then I would be a victim of passive escapism.

Many women may be involved in passive escapism through an obsession with reading romance novels or watching soap operas. I'm not saying you should never read a novel, but I'm talking about a continual lifestyle commitment as a way to escape from stress. If you want to read something occasionally or go to a movie occasionally to get away from a stressful situation to relax, that's okay. There's nothing wrong with that, but I'm talking about using these things as stress management techniques in an extreme way—passive escapism.

So to recap: alcohol and drug abuse, manipulation of people, sexual cheating, job slavery, and passive escapism. Here's what I want you to see. When your reactions to stress are at normal levels, and you try to cope by using SMTs—stress management techniques—that's OK. It helps to find ways of coping with stress. But when you try to cope with stress in an obsessive way that injures your closest relationships and distances you from real, honest involvement in reality—then you are getting into dangerous territory. You're trying to cope, but your coping becomes killing.

STRESS OVERLOAD

Ron Ball has a theory that sometimes we get so stressed-out that we feel like we're continually in an extreme situation. Ron calls this "stress overload." At these times your internal body stress mechanisms seem to get stuck. You can't relax.

Your emotions are going wild. Your body is in rebellion. Even so, you can't shut yourself down. You are tired, but you can't sleep. You need nourishment, but you aren't hungry.

This is a dangerous situation, and maybe because of your interest in bettering yourself and becoming successful, you will at some point in your life be a victim of stress overload. Let me explain to you more of what happens to you during stress overload and what you can do about it:

1. *The normal stress management techniques don't work anymore.* If after exercise or improving your diet or taking a vacation, you still are in the throes of stress tension, it is a sure sign that you're suffering from stress overload.

2. *You find you are victimized by chronic depression.* Chronic depression is like a chronic low-grade fever. You can still function and still do your basic responsibilities, but you don't feel that good. It's like a low-grade fever that keeps you from being at your best. This too is a sign, I believe, of stress overload.

3. *You find that you no longer feel any great passion for anything.* This could happen in any area—in your work, in sex, eating, TV shows, friends—you don't feel any passion for them any longer. It's as if your emotions are drained out, and you don't have anything more to give. When this gets really serious is when it applies to life in general—when you don't feel any passion for life— and you go days, weeks, and months living mechanically, going through the motions. You've

lost your joy for life. This is a serious sign of stress overload.

4. *You feel no joy in the simple beauties of life.* You go outside and it's been a rainy, drab, dreary week, and you get up the next morning and go outside. The sun is shining, the clouds have cleared, a fresh breeze is blowing, it's warmed up 15 degrees. Normally, that would put you on top of the world. You'd have a jump in your step, and you'd be ready to meet the challenge of the day. But even that doesn't help you any longer. You don't feel any appreciation for the simple joys of life.

5. *You find that you're getting outraged over trivial things.* You have become, what one psychologist calls, an "anger addict." Your stress mechanism is stuck. Your inner pressures blow up at the wrong times. Your outrage toward something trivial is left-over anger about something significant, but it's venting at an inappropriate time and place.

6. *You have lost your sense of humor about yourself.* One of the great signs of mental health is humor, and especially the ability to laugh at yourself and not take yourself too seriously. When you take life with a great seriousness, and you can't laugh about yourself, it's a sign of stress overload.

7. *You find that you are in what psychologists call a "malaise."* It's almost as if you are living in an emotional swamp. You're living in psychological quicksand; it just sucks you down. A malaise makes you walk through life like an emotional

zombie. You don't have any vitality, and you're characterized by indecisiveness. Your just floating in slow motion.

Winston Churchill, whom most of you think of as a great leader of our century, a man who led a country in a time of dark war and conflict, a man of great stability and emotional strength actually fought many tough battles with depression. There were several stages in his life when his depression, malaise, feeling of worthlessness became so deep and pronounced that he called it "the black dog." His wife and friends would see that something was happening to him. Churchill would say, "It's the black dog. The black dog is back." Churchill was very dramatic with language, and his reference to the black dog is what I'm describing right here. It was depression in his life coming from a prolonged overload of stress.

OK, so that's stress overload. The black dog is following you. What do you do about it? Let me give you some things that have helped me in my life. I believe they can help you too:

First, you need to back off. Don't try harder. That created your stress in the first place. One of the great Christian leaders in the last century is a man named Lyman Beecher. Reverend Beecher was a hard driver, one of the hardest workers of his generation. He was a leader in spiritual matters, Christian evangelism, and he was involved in some of the great universities and seminaries of his day. His children said that their dad would become so wiped out by stress that the only way he could cope would be by chopping wood. For days he would chop wood. He did mindless, emotion-less, mechanical work until he was worn out physically. Then he would sleep for several days and rest from all his vigorous labor. Slowly, gradually, he'd begin to come out of it.

Now I'm not telling you to chop wood! But pay attention to this man's wisdom. He realized that his stress at times became so great that the worst thing for him to do was to add on more pressure. If he would begin to burn out, he would simply back off from all his preaching engagements and take a break from the passion of his life, which was evangelism. Remember, if your stress mechanism is stuck, you've got to get it unstuck, and the worst thing for you to do is to plunge deeper and create more stress and pressure. Learn to back off.

Second, when you feel stress overload, do the opposite of the pressures you feel. I mean this, of course, within moral limits. If your tendency is to be faithful to your wife, I'm not telling you to do the opposite and go cheat on her! But I mean that if you're becoming compulsive about your work and you work at home three hours every night after supper on paperwork—if you've gotten to the point where you can't stop, do the opposite—just stop and don't do it. Now you'll say, "Well, I've got to get those reports done." Listen, you have to put things in perspective. Are the reports really more important than your health, your well-being, your family? No. So do the opposite of your stress tendency. Instead of doing those reports, spend time with your family. Get some rest. Read a book. Relax.

Finally, deal with your guilt. So much stress is caused by guilt. We feel guilty about our lives, our standards, our lack of accomplishments and we stress ourselves in order to escape from the guilt we feel. I heard of a woman recently who was trying to help a member of her family who was very ill. The situation was grave, and really required professional help. But this woman, feeling guilty for neglecting her relative in the past, felt that she should take on the nursing and care taking responsibilities herself. It was not the sensible, logical decision, but she was blinded by her own guilt. She took on an incredible stress in order to compensate for her guilt feelings.

Well, there is no way in one short chapter I can offer solutions to your personal stress situation. I have here just tried to share some of the thoughts and strategies that have helped me and my coauthor, Ron Ball. I trust they're of some help to you as well.

Again, let me just say that stress is a part of life. Everyone feels it. Everyone has it. The mark of a millionaire is what he does about it.

NINE
A MILLIONAIRE
PRESENTS HIMSELF WELL

One thing you notice when you observe a group of successful people is quite simply that they tend to look good. They have a pleasing, crisp, successful-looking appearance. Now the cynical thing that some people would say is that, of course, successful people can afford to buy nice clothes in order to look good. But, when you look at the situation more closely, you realize that what you see in the image of successful people isn't just fine clothing, but something more—an inner attractiveness that comes through to the outer image.

I will write about outward appearance later in this chapter and offer some practical ideas and suggestions, but really, the more important issue is who you are inside. Because it is your character and perception of yourself that will do the most in communicating an attractive image to other people.

THE INNER YOU

No matter how much you work on your outer appearance—your professional appearance—it's not enough if the inner you, the real you, is not in good shape. I want to deal with several areas that can be hindrances to the real you coming out. There are certain things that can be daily enemies that defeat you and can communicate badly to other people. There are certain inner problems that can stop you cold in your tracks and keep you from being the success that you hope to be.

Let's take a look at these inner problems:

1. Crowd comfort. Do you give in to the pressures of people around you? Do you depend too much on the security, warmth, and comfort of a crowd? Does your need for belonging hinder you from taking a risk and stepping out when the time comes? This is known in psychology as "herd security." Crowd comfort is wanting to be in the middle of a warm, happy herd and being content with your anonymity.

The only problem is you're in the middle of a slow, lazy, going-nowhere herd. You know by now that Winston Churchill is one of my heroes. Let me quote him again. He once said that the difference between a great man and a mediocre man is the willingness to take risks and stand by them. I heard a motivational speaker say the power of making a success of your life is the power of commitment: Make a commitment. Make it *your* commitment. Die by your commitment. Crowd comfort fights the commitment-making process. It lulls you to sleep. It's a sedative, a depressant. Do you want to continue to be a cow in the cattle or do you want to be a leader of the herd?

Let me put it bluntly: You will never reach the heights of achievement if you compromise for the security of crowd comfort. So no matter what kind of person you want to project, if you are weak and insecure on the inside so that you need great doses of crowd comfort to keep you going, you will fail to be what you can be in your life.

Harry Truman faced one of the greatest crises of his presidency when he had to fire Douglas MacArthur. Now whatever you think about MacArthur or Truman, it took a lot of guts for Truman to do it. MacArthur was the great leader of his generation militarily. He was awesomely popular, and he was also insubordinate to the president. He was causing great difficulty in the Korean War. And Truman made the tough, politically unpopular decision to be a leader. He fired MacArthur. It took tremendous courage. He broke out of the political crowd that told Truman, "Don't you touch MacArthur. He's our hero." And yet Truman knew that for the sake of national security, for the welfare of our country, and for the future of our action in Korea, he had to do it. If you're going to be successful and project the image of success to other people, you've got to break away from the compromise of crowd comfort.

A feeling of powerlessness. If you have a great sense of powerlessness on the inside, it doesn't matter how much you try to project on the outside, you're always going to short circuit yourself. You're always going to stop yourself short of what you could become. According to one major sociological study from the University of Pennsylvania, the middle class in America and the lower class in America both are filled with great anger and great depression. Here's their explanation, and it makes sense. They say that depression is really unresolved anger that's bottled up inside of you. All of these middle class and lower class people have depression because they have unresolved anger, and the reason they have unresolved anger is that they feel powerless.

Some of you are in dead-end jobs and you feel powerless. Some of you feel like the government is unresponsive and you feel powerless. Some of you cannot touch God and you feel powerless. Some of your marriages are falling apart and you feel powerless. All this creates anger. When you bottle up the anger, it becomes unresolved anger, and it produces depression. So here you are wanting to dress right and look right and appear right and be professional, but you have this depression, this unresolved anger, this feeling of powerlessness, and you cannot produce the outer image that you want to produce because you feel all this powerlessness and weakness on the inside.

You need to change yourself. You need to do something to change your situation, to attack it. You need to attack the problem that is haunting you and pressuring you and smothering you. You need to eliminate the feeling of powerlessness. No matter what kind of image you try to project, it is useless if you feel so powerless on the inside.

It's so amazing how many people will give up so much for so-called job security. They're safe and secure in their jobs for life, but they're powerless, depressed, and lifeless. Many people feel powerless because they are trying to be what someone else wants them to be. Listen, don't live your life for your father or your mother. Don't live your life for your teacher or for somebody else. Find what God wants you to do, and do it.

Phony effort. You can work really hard at projecting a right image, but if you are putting in a lot of phony effort in order not to do the real job, then you're in trouble before you ever get started.

Let me explain this. Do you realize that you can get so busy doing unnecessary work, doing empty, useless work, that you can use that as an excuse for not plunging in and doing the real job, doing what really needs to be done? You can tell yourself, "I've got to file all these papers." Well, that's great, but maybe to succeed you really need to make twenty crucial phone calls. Forget the files and do the phone calls. But here's the problem: you're doing the files because you're afraid to do the phone calls. You're nervous talking to people on the phone. So you'll do all kinds of work, and then when somebody comes and says something about those phone calls, you look at them and say, "Phone calls? Oh, I'd love to do it. I really would do it, but I've got all this filing to do." You see, this is just a way of putting up a smoke screen so people won't see that you're really not wanting to make the sacrifices and take the risks to do the real job.

Let me be very honest with you. There's a great deal that you do that is just laziness in disguise. A lot of your work is really work to camouflage the truth—that you don't want to do the real job.

Here's another "chopping-wood" story to illustrate my point. I know of a man who all the time goes outside to chop wood. He tells his wife that he didn't have time to fix things around the house because he had to chop wood. But they had plenty of wood. More than they could use. The real truth is that he enjoys chopping wood. He doesn't enjoy plumbing or repairing things around the house. He would work alright, but it was really phony work that wasn't accomplishing anything useful. You need to do what is truly the most productive thing you can do. Don't camouflage your fears or laziness with false phony effort.

Hiding behind status. I heard the story of a woman in another state who was highly qualified and well trained for a particular job. The only problem was that her job did not pay much money. It was a glamour job, a high-profile job with a lot of status. But the pay was low. She loved her job, but she always complained about the low pay. She finally put out some resumes and checked out the job market. Well, she was so well trained that three or four other companies contacted her, offering her different jobs with less glamour and less of a title, but more money. One of the offers was double the amount that she was making at that point. She turned down every job offer and chose to stay with that status job. Now, that wouldn't be wrong if that's what she really wanted. The problem was that later she was still complaining about not making enough money, and then she started blaming other people. She blamed her boss, saying he should pay her more, that he didn't pay her what she was worth. But she made a choice. That choice was status, glamour, and appearance instead of substance. She wanted prestige instead of money. And to be very honest with you, she got what she asked for.

Some of you are hiding behind status as well. You like the strokes you get in your current job. You enjoy the status that you've earned over the years. But you aren't going anywhere. You're hiding behind false status, hiding from the risks you need to take to go into a new direction.

It doesn't matter what you try to project through your outward appearance—the type of jacket you wear, the type of dress you put on. All that is not enough. People will see the inner you somehow, no matter how hard you try to hide those parts of yourself. You've got to be the right kind of person with the proper, winning attitude on the inside.

Lying to yourself. You need to tell yourself the truth and face up to what you really want in life and what you're willing to do to get it. Again, make friends with facts, this time, facts about yourself. Your actions will prove the truth about you.

You're a product of your choices. Accept that. If you aren't further along than you are in a particular area, it's because you have made choices that have contributed to that. You are a product of what you've chosen. Don't lie to yourself. Don't blame someone else. Don't throw excuses around. They are like nooses around your neck. You need to realize that lying to yourself will only stop you from being the man or woman of success that you need to be. And those inner problems show on the outside.

One of the greatest examples I have ever heard of this is a man who was President Kennedy's personal envoy to the country of Laos in 1961, before the Vietnam War erupted. President Kennedy sent this man to try to untangle some negotiations that had gotten hopelessly sidetracked. Kennedy looked at him and said, "Do you know how tough this is going to be?" And the man replied, "I understand." Kennedy told him not to lie to himself. He had chosen this man because he always faced reality and always faced up to the truth. So it was that this envoy embarked on this assignment with a great commitment to do the job and solve these problems. He flew to Laos, got off an airplane, and immediately an American reporter met him and asked him a question: "You know it's going to be hard in these negotiations. They appear to be hopelessly stalled. Are you pessimistic or optimistic?" The envoy looked at the reporter and replied, "I am neither. I am determined."

Listen, you've got to be determined to tell yourself the truth, even if it hurts. You need to face the facts.

Are you compromising for crowd comfort? Are you filled with depression and unresolved anger and powerlessness and unwilling to do anything about it? Are you covering up your true effort with false and phony work? Are you deceiving yourself about yourself? If you truly want to make a good impression upon people, take care of tidying up your inner wardrobe before you spend money on your outer wardrobe.

Friends, you're not trying to fool people and make them think you're something you're not. You simply want to use your outward appearance to project who you really are. That's means the real you—the inner you—must be a person you want others to see.

THE OUTER YOU

How you dress does project something about you. Do you realize that in order to project the right image, you have to be aware of how you're communicating things visually? Let me suggest some guidelines about dressing for success in the nineties:

Think classic. Remember that the classic styles stay in style. A classic is something that has stood the test of time. Do you realize that Brooks Brothers suits still offer for sale in their store some suit styles for men that are basically unchanged since the early 1800s? Now, there are a few minor variations here or there, but still the same basic suits sell in the 1980s. You'll never go wrong if you buy something that is classic.

Avoid fads. Fads lead to failure. A fad is something that the fashion industry produces to get you to spend more money on their product. Also a fad tends to go out of style as fast as it comes in style. And it's funny that it seems no one's around to tell you when the fad is passe. Most fad fashions are loners—that is, they can't be matched to other items in your wardrobe. So, generally it's best to avoid fad fashions entirely.

Keep your clothes neat and pressed. I think you'll agree with me that the one thing you notice about successful people is that they always look fresh and crisp in their wardrobe. Sometimes the link to greater success is simply a better relationship with your dry cleaner! There is nothing that hurts a an image worse than unpolished shoes or a wrinkled shirt with bad collars and bad cuffs. Get them starched and make them crisp and clean.

Make sure your clothes fit well. Spend a little more for good tailoring. The few dollars extra will bring in many times that through the better image you will project. If you have heavier hips, you don't want them bulging out to the center of your coat. You don't want your suit coat bunching up in the back. If you're a short woman, you don't want to wear a suit coat that is too short because it will make you look squat and heavy. Maximize your good features; minimize your physical shortcomings.

Avoid the four basic clothing traps. Susan Bixler writes about these in her book *The Professional Image.* She lists four clothing traps to avoid: (1) The "sale sign" trap—if it's on sale buy it. No, don't buy it unless you really need it, can afford it, and can use it. You wouldn't believe what hangs in some people's closets that they never wear because they bought it on sale. (2) The designer label trap—it must be good if it has a designer label and costs more money. Those things are faddish. The designer label trap is a product of advertising, does not ensure any better quality, and can cost you a lot of money. (3) The "in a hurry" trap. You're in a hurry, you have to pick up something for a dinner tonight, you have to buy now. Consequently, you don't think it through. Consequently, you make a poor choice and get a bad fit. (4) The "no planning" trap. If you don't plan what you're going out to buy, you will almost always buy clothes you don't need and that don't work well together, and you will no doubt spend lots more money than if you had planned ahead.

Choose quality even if it means you pay a little more and purchase fewer items. Quality clothes last longer and are less expensive in the long run. They also look better and press easier. Quality shows. Consider natural fabrics as much as you can. Buy quality.

Dress in such a way that you can forget about what you're wearing. If you are uncomfortable in a new outfit, then there's probably something wrong. It may not fit well, or it may not be appropriate, or it may be too complicated a combination of clothes. Dress simply enough and properly enough for each occasion that your clothes become a natural-feeling part of you.

Let me go back now to the first principle. I've really been saying there are two issues regarding appearance: cosmetic and character. The character is who you really are on the inside. Don't become so obsessed with an outward image that you neglect the real you, the quality character traits that make you attractive to other people. Clothing can never be a substitute for lack of character or poor performance. If there is a contradiction between your appearance and who you really are inside, eventually people will perceive you as a phony. The real secret is to genuinely love other people and care about them and treat them with respect. Dress the best way you can to present yourself effectively, but concentrate on your inner wardrobe even more.

TEN
A MILLIONAIRE
SEEKS GOOD COUNSEL

This mark of a millionaire may surprise you. After all, aren't millionaires the ones who have the answers? Aren't they the people who are counseling others?

Well, yes and no. Of course, most millionaires have learned a thing or two on the way to making their first million. Successful people do dispense their own formulas for success and getting ahead, providing counsel for those who are looking for it.

But one thing you notice when you examine the lives of these people—they seek help and counsel from trusted aides and advisers. Millionaires know enough to know they don't know enough. They hire people who are experts in those areas that they themselves aren't expert in. Successful people understand the value of good counsel.

LEARNING TO ACCEPT ADVICE

The first step for many people is developing the openness to receiving advice. A lot of people don't want to seek help; they want to do everything themselves.

Ron Ball tells a personal story that illustrates this well. One month after he and his new bride, Amy, were married, they decided that they needed to buy a new desk. Ron didn't ask anybody's advice about what desk to buy; he went out and bought a kit at K-Mart. On the box it said that if the customer would just follow certain directions, the desk could be easily assembled. When he returned home, Amy met him at the door full of excitement and asked, "Alright, so where's the desk?" Ron showed her the box and said with great confidence that it was a kit that he could easily put together. He proceeded to open the kit and take out all the pieces, laying all the parts on the floor. At the bottom of the box was something crucial. A sheet of directions. Ron, thinking the task was a cinch, took the directions, crumpled them up, and tossed them aside. He thought, *Hey, I'm a college graduate. I don't need directions.* Of course, in his own way he was saying he didn't need help or advice. So he started to work. Now on the outside of the box in big letters it said that the whole desk could be ready for use in thirty minutes. But Ron struggled with the kit for an hour, then two hours, then three hours. He worked until four in the morning and finally gave up, only to tackle it again the next day. After four-and-a-half days he finally realized that something was badly wrong! He went next door to a neighboring student and borrowed a drill and a huge roll of masking tape. He drilled holes into the desk, drove nails into it, put masking tape around it, and although it wobbled and it shook, the desk was finally completed.

Ron finally realized that he should have read the directions. Unfortunately his pride and self-reliance got in the way, and he wasted a lot of valuable personal time because he didn't seek counsel. He didn't read the directions.

LEARNING TO AVOID BAD COUNSEL

Another problem many people have is that they tend to find bad counsel instead of good, right counsel. There happens to be a lot of bad counsel available to people these days, and it's important to know what it is, in order to avoid it. Let me suggest to you five characteristics of bad counsel:

1. Bad counsel is negative. Negative counsel comes from well-intentioned people who keep telling you what *not* to do. "Don't try..." "Don't do..." "Don't reach for...." They always tell you no when you need to hear a yes. I'm not saying that counsel can never tell you something you don't want to hear--sometimes it must, but then it should provide you with a positive direction to replace the negative warning. Counsel that is always negative is bad counsel. Avoid it.

2. Bad counsel is almost always over-cautious.

Bad counsel will warn you about every danger, caution you about taking any risk. It tends to be extremely conservative. It makes you afraid to move, wary of the consequences of any action. Bad counsel tells you not to build a business because of the financial risks, or not to grow too big or else you'll be a materialistic person, or don't try to accomplish something that might make someone mad at you. Again, it's not that caution can't be valuable advice, but that counsel that is entirely cautious can paralyze you.

3. Bad counsel is oversensitive about other people's opinions. If you're getting counsel from someone, and they're always counseling you to be careful of what so-and-so thinks, take it with a grain of salt. Remember that if you accomplish anything significant, someone is bound to criticize.

4. Negative counsel creates confusion. Instead of helping you think clearly and get your goal in focus, bad counsel confuses you and blurs your vision for the future. Counsel should be clear and logical.

5. Bad counsel violates the principles of the Bible. I don't make any apology for that statement because I believe those principles are basic to your life and your success. To go against the teachings of the Bible is to jeopardize everything you love and everything you hope for. If you violate the principles that God has given, then you endanger your family, your children, and yourself. You play a fool's game of high risk with God. You want counsel that's consistent with what the Bible really teaches.

LEARNING TO RECOGNIZE GOOD COUNSEL

Good counsel can change your life. It can make you a more complete person, more clearly aware of your strengths and weaknesses. Let's look at some of the characteristics of good counsel:

1. *Good counsel will discipline your natural tendencies.* A business associate of mine once said, "I've learned something about negotiation. When you get to the point in a negotiation where some things are just not negotiable, then you need to tell people that this is totally unacceptable."

Ron Ball got an opportunity to test this advice recently. He and his wife, Amy, were in Atlanta and decided to do some shopping. Amy found a couple of pairs of shorts and two tops. There was a third pair of shorts and top that she really liked but were expensive. Ron and Amy decided that they would buy just the two and not the third. Ron paid, the outfits were placed in a bag, and Ron and Amy went back to their hotel.

In the middle of the night, Ron awoke and suddenly remembered that he had left not with two outfits, but three. Checking the receipt, he discovered he had paid for it even though they never wanted to buy the third outfit. The next day he returned to the store. It featured a big sign that said the store didn't give refunds, only credits. He asked the salesperson, "Excuse me, we didn't mean to buy this. It was put in our bag by mistake; we were charged for it, but we didn't want to buy it." She told him that the policy of the store was no refunds. She said she was sorry, but there was nothing she could do.

Now Ron says that at that point the sanguine part of him, the part of him that wants everybody to like Ron Ball, emerged strongly. It was his natural tendency to say to her, "Oh, well, that's OK, it's not your fault. I guess we can use the outfit anyway." But he remembered the counsel of my business associate regarding negotiation. He decided to try it out. Ron looked at the salesperson and said, "I'm sorry, but that is totally unacceptable."

He argued his position with her for almost two hours. She finally tracked down the manager, to whom Ron reiterated, "It's your mistake. I want a refund. Credits are totally unacceptable." Finally the store manager relented and gave him his money.

Here's what I want you to see. Ron was in a situation where he needed to discipline his natural tendencies. His natural tendency was "Don't worry about it, forget the money." He learned how to negotiate something that his natural tendency wouldn't have allowed him to do previously. Good counsel will discipline your natural tendencies.

2. *Good counsel will fill in the gaps of your experience in your knowledge.* That's why good tapes and books are so vital. Good counsel will fill up information gaps. We all have gaps and need gap-fillers, and you get gap-fillers through good counseling. Successful people don't know everything. They do surround themselves with people who supplement their lack of knowledge in certain areas.

3. *Good counseling will overcome weaknesses in*

your life. Inc. magazine told a wonderful story by Tom Petters. Peters is probably the most famous management consultant in the world, coauthor of *In Search of Excellence.* Peters wrote about a recent experience:

"I went home recently, turned on my answering machine, and Frank Perdue of Perdue Chickens was trying to get in touch with me. He had been calling me for weeks, and I kept sending word back to him that I was busy, and that I would try to get back to him. But I never answered his call. One day last week I walked in, flipped on the machine, and Frank Perdue's voice said, 'Listen Peters, if you're going to yap about excellence and service, why don't you try doing it for a change? Good-bye.'"

"So here was Tom Peters, a famous man who had written a book about excellence and service, and Frank Perdue said that if he was going to be so sloppy in answering his messages to count him out. You know what good counseling does sometimes—it stings, cuts, and hurts, but it will make you better. Do you want to be better? Better than you've ever been? You've got to have good counsel.

4. Good counseling will control your ego. It's easy, when you're at the top, to get full of yourself and to think that you have some special genius for success. We've already seen in this book that success doesn't just happen—it takes hard work, planning, and the constant pursuit of a dream. But when you get some success—and maybe you're in this position now—it's easy to get egotistical about it. Good counsel will remind you that your success comes from hard work, from tapping into other people and treating them well, from good planning. Good counsel has the guts to take you down a notch when you need it.

FINDING THE RIGHT COUNSELOR

One of the hardest things to do is find the right people to be your counselors. Let me suggest to you ten characteristics of a good counselor. These ten things have helped me immensely in my own life as I've sought good people to assist me in my work.

First, a good counselor is honest to the core. You don't want people who play games with you. You need counselors who will be absolutely honest. This is hard for most of us because we tend to select friends (and counselors) who make us feel good about ourselves. We like to be complimented and supported. But it is through those kinds of people that little lies and untruths are told. It isn't intentional, but it's also not the kind of direct honesty you need in a counselor.

Second, you have to have a counselor with a consistent track record. You should like a person's background, his history, his previous employment, his family life. You want someone who has been consistent in life and who will be consistent with you.

Third, you want to find a counselor who seeks

the same kind of success you want. That's critical. If you and your counselor have different goals, different visions of what constitutes success, then you'll wind up with bad advice. At least bad for you. It's best if you can find someone who shares your dream.

Fourth, a counselor has to have the knowledge you know you need. You're looking for someone to fill in the gaps of your knowledge. Again the tendency here is to get close to people who share your knowledge base. It's natural for us to avoid people who are knowledgeable in ways we aren't. You have to overcome those tendencies and seek people who are strong in areas you aren't.

Fifth, you want somebody who really, really cares about you. You've got to find somebody who really has your best interests at heart. You want someone who will ultimately stand by your side during the tough times. Those counselors are hard to find, but when found, they're worth their weight in gold.

Sixth, you need someone who is willing to understand your personality. Each of us has his quirks and idiosyncrasies. That's what makes us interesting. It's also what makes us frustrating to other people. A good counselor is one who understands your personality and who mediates in situations where you are in conflict with other people.

Seventh, you need to look for a counselor who is practical, flexible, and filled with common sense. A good counselor won't get carried away by idealism and always has his feet on the ground. You need common sense to steer you away from frivolous endeavors and to refocus you in productive, realistic directions.

Eighth, look for a counselor with a positive bent. You need someone who looks at your dream believing it can be done. We'll talk about the importance of a positive attitude in another chapter, but for now, let me simply suggest to you that someone who is consistently negative is someone who will make a bad counselor.

Ninth, you need a counselor who knows when to keep his mouth shut. Now, I don't say that disrespectfully. What I mean is that good counselors don't gossip. They don't betray your trust. They don't leak confidential information to other people.

Finally, I believe you need a counselor who has a right relationship with God and a strong moral foundation. In this day and age, the roads of business and commerce are filled with the potholes of greed and corruption. White-collar crime has gotten a lot of press recently. I doubt that anyone intends at the start to do anything wrong or immoral. It starts with little ways of getting an advantage, actions that are legal but maybe slightly unethical. It grows into something more and something illegal. It takes a strong person to avoid those holes in the road. A good counselor—one who will say to you sometime, "That would work, but that would be wrong."—is the kind of person you need around you.

Let me say one thing in conclusion. In a nutshell, you want a counselor who will tell you the

truth. The truth is sometimes good news, sometimes bad news. It is sometimes positive, sometimes negative. It is always moral. You need
someone who will be an honest mirror, reflecting
the real facts about who you are and what you are
doing.

ELEVEN
A MILLIONAIRE
THINKS POSITIVELY

Ron tells a story about his daughter, Allison. One day he took her to a park called Kids Fest, which is a big game area. Ron was standing beside a man and his wife, and their small boy was climbing some ropes and was having trouble. He was only about three years old, and he was struggling to get up these big, heavy ropes. At one point he had slipped three times and was trying to get up again. Even though he wasn't having much success, it seemed as if he was having a good time. But at this point, the boy's father yelled in a booming voice, "Hey, Ryan, come on fellow. You can do it." And then Ryan slipped again. And then the father yelled, "I knew it. You're nothing but a dummy." Ryan's mother turned to this father and said, "Please don't call him that. Don't say that to him." And the father said, "Alright, you're not a dummy. So you're an idiot, just like your mother." And here was this three-year-old boy. You know that boy heard that and internalized it. Something died inside that boy. And here was this dad who had no right to be a dad. I really believe that somebody should have lovingly kicked that man's teeth in. He never should have done that to his son.

The problem is, most of us have had that same experience at some point in our lives. Some of us have heard words like that over and over again. We've been programmed negatively, to think negative thoughts about ourselves.

One of the significant characteristics of successful people seems to be that they think positively about life and about themselves.

Now perhaps you are thinking that it's easy to think highly of yourself when you're wealthy and successful. Perhaps, but I don't think in most cases that the wealth and the success came first. I've seen it over and over again—when a person changes his attitude from being negative to being positive, then good things happen and success comes one's way.

PRIDE VERSUS SELF-RESPECT

Do you understand the distinction between pride and self-respect? There is a pride that says, "I don't need God and I don't need other people." It is much the same concept as in the word 'egotism.' For example when the Bible says, "Pride comes before a fall"—it's warning you that arrogant egotism will wreck your life. If you don't think you need God, you've got another thing coming. If you don't need other people, wake up—you need everybody. The Bible is condemning arrogant egotistical pride.

On the other hand, the Bible does not condemn a healthy pride, a view of yourself that is honest and right. In fact, the very word *humble* in the Greek language simply means "an accurate appraisal of yourself." It means that what you think and say about yourself is accurate.

Let me tell you a story about one of the great preachers of the church. He was frequently compared to William Jennings Bryan, the great political orator of several generations ago. This man, Dr. Morrison, was preaching with a number of other well-known community leaders. They were sharing the platform for a week in a large crusade. And one evening after all of the sessions had been completed, Dr. Morrison and four of these leaders were chatting. One of them said, "Let's pray for tomorrow's services." So all four of them knelt and prayed, and one of them began to pray a very pious, spiritual prayer. He said, "O heavenly Father, I want to thank you for what you're doing in this crusade. And you know that I have no ability to preach or to speak, that none of us have any ability at all. We cannot do anything, we don't even know how to preach. . . ." It was at this point that Dr. Morrison got fed up; he just couldn't take it any more. He stood up and said, "John, don't lie to God." And all the preachers were startled and looked at Morrison. Morrison said again, "Don't lie to God. You know you can preach. God gave you the ability. Don't lie to God. Don't dishonor God by putting yourself down."

Most of us have been programmed to think it's best if we frequently cut ourselves down to size. We have learned to believe, wrongly, that it's a characteristic of humility and that it's a more attractive personality trait. But it really isn't.

How do you respond to an honest compliment? If I said to you, "That's a very attractive dress—I like that," do you become embarrassed and reply, "Oh, well, no. I got this dress at K-Mart eight years ago, and it's really not very good at all"? What you've done is not only put yourself down, but you've put me down because I like the dress. You have criticized my taste. Listen, you're not helping anybody by offering a false reaction to a compliment. Why not just say, "Thank you. I like it too."?

This misunderstanding regarding the difference between pride and healthy self-respect is probably one of the biggest hindrances toward a positive attitude and a real roadblock to acheiving success. In order to become successful, you must develop a healthy pride, a strong sense of self-respect.

TEN STEPS TO A POSITIVE ATTITUDE
I have good news. Western civilization has given you a great psychological gift. Do you know what it is? It's called the New Year. It means at the end of the old year you can bury the trash, take out the garbage, and get ready for things to be better. I'm

going to give you a ten-point program to break the power of past failures and regrets and to help you build a positive attitude. Maybe you can use these on New Year's Eve, but you certainly don't have to wait to put them into action!

1. Take charge of your life. Stop blaming somebody else. It's your life, and chances are you've had something to do with your present situation. Accept that. Then let go of it. Admit you are responsible. Take charge. Take charge of your business now. Take charge of your debts now. Take charge of your future now. Take charge of your marriage now. Take charge of your life now. This is the first rung on the ladder to positive thinking in your life.

2. Seize the moments in your life. Don't wait for something to happen to you. Don't wait to live. Live now. Ron Ball told of being with a great evangelist from Argentina named Luis Palau. He had picked up Luis from the airport to meet Charles Stanley, a pastor, in Atlanta. He was driving him and Luis said, "Ron, you want to preach, to teach, to tell people about Jesus Christ.— And Ron said, "Yes, that's what I want more than anything else in the world." And Luis said, "Listen, if you go into a town and almost nobody comes to hear you, seize the moment. Give them your best anyway. If you do that every time, then sooner or later, God's going to give you success. That one person you think is a nobody could be somebody who will come to Jesus Christ."

Did you see Robin Williams in the movie *Dead Poets Society*? A powerful film. Remember the scene where he takes these cocky teenage students who think they know everything and brings them into the hallway to show them a whole line of paintings? He says, "Do you see these paintings, these pictures? These are the graduating classes before you, fifty, sixty, and seventy years ago in this school. They're all dead now, and if they could say one thing to you who are freshmen in this school, do you know what they would say? They'd say, 'Seize the day.'"

That's what you have to do. You can't wait for life to happen to you. You can't expect life, when it does happen to you, to be what you need or dream of. Seize the moment.

3. *Learn to correct the correctable and forget the uncorrectable.* If something has to be changed that is standing in the way of your building a successful life, change it. If you can't change it, forget about it. If you've failed in your business because you've just been too stubborn to get right counsel from books and tapes, then change, force yourself to swallow your self-reliance, and listen to those tapes and read those books. Correct what is correctable. If you have failed because there has been an economic lull in your region, then shrug your shoulders and let go of it. There's nothing you can do about that anyway. Put your energy into something else. Forget the uncorrectable.

4. *Purify your vision.* I was in Ogden, Utah, and Ron came to see me. I asked him if he wanted something to eat. I said I was going to get a turkey sandwich, and Ron said he wanted a hamburger,

but he said he would just get a turkey sandwich too. So we called up room service and ordered two turkey sandwiches, no gravy, just lean white meat, nothing else. About this time, I said, "Could you wait a minute?" And I looked at Ron and said, "You don't want the turkey sandwich do you?" And Ron replied, "No, I really want a hamburger, but it's OK. I'll eat the turkey sandwich." And I called back and said, "One turkey sandwich, one hamburger." And I hung up and said, "Ron, if you want a hamburger and you eat a turkey sandwich to make me happy, all you'll do is eat the turkey sandwich and then go stuff yourself on a hamburger later. Ron, if I ever ask you what your dream is, tell me what you want, not what you think I want to hear. If it's not what you want, you won't do what it takes to get it."

So, to develop a positive attitude, make sure you're clear on the dream you said you dreamed at first. Make sure it's what you really want. Once you purify your vision, you will find your attitude changing from one of regret into one of new enthusiasm.

5. Develop positive memory control. Your memories will kill you if they're negative and you wallow in them. Ron told me a good story recently:

I was watching a football game three or four weeks ago. My family—including my mother-in-law, father-in-law, sister-in-law, brother-in-law, and my wife—are New York Giants fans because they all lived in New Jersey, and the

Giants were playing the San Francisco 49ers. The 49ers had a lead, but the Giants had the ball deep in their own end zone. I was on the phone, watching this with mute on the TV. Now, I was listening to the person on the other end, but I was sort of watching the game too, and then it happened. Right in front of my eyes, Phil Simms threw a pass he should never have thrown. It was intercepted, and with that he lost the game. I watched Simms walk over to Bill Parcells, the Giants head coach, and Sims was so mad, and you could read their lips, and Parcells looked at Sims and stopped him and said, "Forget it." Simms said something really angry to Parcells that I couldn't hear, but Parcells grabbed his quarterback, wheeled him around, and said, "I said to forget it." And then he walked off. And then I said to the person on the other line, "I think I've got my illustration for Friday night!"

You know why? Sometimes after you've failed, the best thing you can do is just forget it and go on.

As it turned out, the Giants lost that game but came back and won their divisional championship. You see, if Simms had not forgotten about his interception, it would have crippled him as a player.

Now, what is it right now that you refuse to forget that cripples you? Do you think you're not worthy to build a distributorship because you've done so bad this past year or you've handled your finances poorly? Forget it. I'm talking freedom here. Forget it. Learn positive memory control.

6. *Let realism rule your emotions.* You should reach for the reachable, but make sure there is some stretch built in. You want to reach for what you can get, but you want to reach for a little more than is easy to get. A part of realism is to always tell yourself the truth. If you lie to yourself, you'll never be who you can be. Always tell yourself the truth—your marriage, your spiritual life, your finances—and you'll find that a positive attitude comes more naturally. You'll believe in yourself because you'll know you're building on truth.

7. *Do an action analysis.* Make sure your actions toward your dream always have action as a result. Otherwise it's like water pouring into a stagnant pond. If the water never goes out, it stinks and does nobody any good. It's like the Dead Sea in Israel. Water flows in from the north, but there's no out-flow in the south, and that's why it's called the Dead Sea. So while you make your plans, make sure they always result in action. Analyze where you want to go, and then go there. Taking this step will propel you into active, positive thinking about your future.

8. *Learn from positive examples of other people.* Let me give you some positive life examples right now, and you'll see my point.

Robert Swanson is the founder of Genentech, the fastest-growing Fortune 500 company in the history of American business. Genentech is a microbiology firm—they're working on research for AIDS and cancer, and they invented artificial insulin that has begun to revolutionize diabetic treatment. Robert Swanson is a tremendous success, but when he was in his twenties he worked for Citibank. A firm called Kleiner & Perkins, whose sole purpose was to raise venture capital for start-up companies, hired him away from Citibank and said, "Go to it, Robert. You've got a great future in Silicon Valley, California." A year later they fired him, and it was the greatest failure of his life, but Robert Swanson didn't dwell on the failure and didn't think negative thoughts and didn't wallow in regret. He said, "I decided it was only going to bring one result in my life—I decided the only thing I would allow it to do was to increase my grit level that much more." And since then he's built the fastest growing Fortune 500 company in America. He succeeded.

When Denis Waitley was in his late thirties he thought his whole life was over. Every dream he had ever dreamed failed to come true, and he decided to do one last thing before he just gave up. He decided to write down some things he had been studying. He put together a manuscript and said, "This is my last hurrah and it's over." He gave it the title, *The Psychology of Winning*, and it became an international bestseller. Denis Waitley right now is one of the most famous motivational speakers in the world.

Harry S. Truman—do you realize he went bankrupt as a farmer? Then he started a store and went bankrupt as a merchant. He didn't enter politics until he was in his forties, and after winning one local election, he ran for reelection and lost. But Harry Truman became president of the United States.

Ray Kroc decided to make a fortune in real estate. On his thirtieth birthday he wrote these words: "I have succeeded in two things. I am stone broke, and I am a total failure." And of course it was Kroc who founded and developed the McDonald's Corporation.

One thing these and others have in common is the ability to remain positive in difficult situations. These were people who failed at one point or another in their lives, but the didn't get down on themselves. They thought positively about the things that could still happen.

9. *Find God's purpose for your life.* It's not enough to do your own thing. Whatever kind of success you make for yourself in this life, it won't count for much in the next life. Jesus said, "What will it profit you if you gain the whole world but lose your soul?" You have to connect with the eternal, and if you want something that will get you out of bed in the morning, find God's purpose for you. Now, that doesn't mean that God's purpose is not financial—and a lot of people think that. But I believe God wants you to be secure financially. I believe he wants you to take care of your family. He wants you to prosper and succeed in balance with other things as long as they stay in balance.

I believe the only way to connect with the eternal is through a personal relationship with Jesus Christ. When you discover that, God will pour his purpose into your soul, and you'll have a power to get you out of bed in the morning when nothing else will.

10. Don't get going, get doing. Nothing is ever done unless you do it. Does that sound dumb to you? Think about it. There's a lot of common sense in common-sense sayings. Nothing is ever done unless you do it. So why don't you set some do-able goals right now? Set a measurable amount of time you're going to give to your business every week. Write down a measurable amount of hours. Say something positive to build the self-esteem of your children every day. Do something romantic, loving, and unexpected for your husband or wife each week. Those are very do-able things. Save 10 percent of your income every month and apply it to debt reduction if you're really in debt. That's do-able. Spend fifteen minutes a day with a positive book. Spend some time each day reading the Bible. That's do-able. All of these things will begin to change you. And as you act, and as you change, your outlook will change too for the better. You'll become a positive thinker, and that will make all the difference.

TWELVE
A MILLIONAIRE
DEVELOPS MATURITY

This chapter should be a good balance to the last one on positive attitudes. That's because in this short chapter I would like to present to you four of the hardest lessons you will need to learn in order to be successful.

LOTTERY FAILURES

Some people's concept of becoming a millionaire is winning the lottery. Getting rich quick. Instantaneous wealth. Well, do you know something? Many people who have won the lottery are today flat broke. They spent their money, squandered it, invested it badly, and once the yearly payments ended, their wealth ended. They were given the millions, but they didn't have the maturity to handle it. They hadn't learned the lessons of success that are necessary not only to make millions, but to *keep* millions.

I believe that when you look at people who have become successful and have stayed successful in their lives, you see a kind of maturity. It's a wisdom that we sometimes see in our grandparents as we're growing up, a steady, mature outlook on life that grows out of experience and sometimes difficulty and pain.

FOUR PRINCIPLES OF DEVELOPING MATURITY

I think we can distill some of those principles of maturity and use them in our own quest for success. Maturity cannot be developed overnight, but it can be developed—and these four lessons are a good beginning.

1. Learn the principle of delayed gratification. Long-term commitment is what it takes to produce results. The average college student right now takes five and a half years to graduate from college. The majority of college graduates today wait until their late twenties before they find themselves and get started building their careers.

It's the difference between short-term and long-term results.

I know of a man who is a financial consultant. He was giving a seminar once and said, "So many of you want to get rich quick, and that's your mistake. Because according to the Bible, you get rich slow." You build, you develop, you save. It takes time. Maturity takes time.

In other books I've talked about the importance of developing a personal financial plan to get out of debt and to save and to invest. I have written about the importance of deciding what you want and what you don't want and sticking to those goals for years and years and years. Now I find that many people can get the planning right, and they may even be able to get out of debt, but what kills them in their quest for financial independence is the long-term commitment. Their resolve breaks down along the way, and they are seduced by advertising to get this or this or this, things that were not a part of the original plan, and suddenly their commitment to independence falters.

The hardest lesson successful people have to learn is that of delayed gratification—waiting for the results of financial wisdom. True wealth does not happen overnight. It comes as a result of a lifetime of planning and saving and investing. It comes from cultivating a dream, putting it into action, and working hard. Most people don't have the patience for that. Those that do, become successful.

2. Learn the earning principle. I've already mentioned the importance of hard work in pursuing your dream. This is another hard lesson many people have to learn. If you're looking to make the most money for the least work, then you're mind set is completely off-track. With that thinking, you will never become successful. Success is based on the principle that wealth is earned and worked for.

Have you seen the wall poster that shows a picture of a man hang-gliding all over the sky? A sunset is the background. The man looks so free like he's having the time of his life. It says on the poster, "You have the power to make your dreams come true. You may have to work for them, however."

3. Learn that life is unfair. One thing I notice about successful people is that they don't always expect life to deal a fair deal. They expect certain things to be unfair. They don't cry and whine when something bad happens; instead they just dig themselves out of it, and start over again.

The truth is that life is often unfair. Natural disasters destroy homes and businesses. The stock market takes a plunge. A traffic jam makes you late for an important business meeting. These are things out of your control, and they seem unfair. They are unfair.

The hard lesson to learn is that unfairness happens. We have to accept it, and move on. Moaning and groaning about those things simply saps your energy. You don't see successful people doing that.

4. Learn from troubles and problems. Don't allow troubles to crush you. You can't afford to allow your troubles to win in your life. A failure is never a failure when you learn from it. Someone once observed, "Great trials often precede great triumphs."

Let me tell you about a man you know. But you probably don't know his background. When he was a young man, he went to the best private school in England. When he was fourteen years old, he made the lowest grades in the history of the school. When he was nineteen, he decided he wanted to go to Sandhurst Military Academy; he applied and failed the entrance examination. He tried again six months later and failed again. He went back, gave it one more shot, and he got in by the skin of his teeth. Then he performed military service. At twenty-five years of age, he decided to go into politics. He ran for Parliament, and he lost. Then he went to cover a war in South Africa, where he was captured. He escaped, came back home, ran for Parliament, and won. Then he began to rise in the ranks of his government until he became what is known in England as the First Lord of the Admiralty, head of the greatest navy in the world. In the process he started the Royal Air Force and invented the tank. This man was brilliant. Then at age forty-one, there was a scandal in his government. He was only indirectly connected to the scandal, but he was thrown out of office in disgrace. He tried to fight back. At age forty-eight he ran for Parliament and lost. At age forty-nine he ran for Parliament and lost. That same year he ran again in another race and barely won, but he was nonetheless back in. He thought then that he would make it, that he was OK. And he started making more money. He was in his fifties and everything looked great. But when he was fifty-four, on the advice of an American friend, he put all his money in the American Stock Market. This was 1929. In October he got the message that he was dead broke. The next year he visited the United States again, stepped out of a taxi cab on what for him was the wrong side of the street, and was hit by a car. He almost died. He lingered for months at the edge of death. During this time, he couldn't make money, and he lost his seat in Parliament. He recovered, and he returned to government, but there was another scandal, and he was thrown out again and became a national joke. Shortly thereafter World War II broke out in Europe. England was suddenly threatened. In 1939 a radio message was broadcast across England. This man's daughter, Margaret, vacationing in Bristol, flipped on the radio, and the news announcer said, "Her Majesty's government has put out an urgent plea for Mr. Winston Churchill to return and take over the government." Do you realize that Winston Churchill, at age sixty-five, had three times more failures than he had successes? He had lost almost everything in his life, and he wrote right before this that he was experiencing what he called "the black dog of depression." Even so, he refused to quit. And it was Winston Churchill's determination to learn from his personal troubles that helped England pull through during one of the darkest periods of the century.

Recently I read a study of people who get into debt and people who don't get into debt. The greatest difference between those who are deep in debt and those who aren't is maturity.

People with the greatest maturity don't get into such personal debt. These people accept the idea that financial success is something that doesn't happen overnight. They have learned that wealth needs to be earned. They have accepted the fact that life isn't always fair, and they've learned from their troubles and mistakes. Finally, now, they are getting themselves out of debt and staying out.

I saw a commercial last year that was terribly blatant in its pitch: "Hey, do you want it now? You don't have to wait. You can get it now. Easy credit. Easy terms. Get it now." A mature person sees through that. Those who aren't mature and haven't learned these hard lessons of success, simply need to do so more growing up.

THIRTEEN
A MILLIONAIRE
IS A PIONEER

Have you experienced the dramatic visual program of the American Adventure at Epcot in Orlando? You sit there in the dark and see this amazing display of American ingenuity and effectiveness. You're thrilled with what's happened, and you realize that people all over the world are getting a new spirit, a new attitude. The lights go down, the curtains go up, and the silhouette of an American patriot soldier—a minuteman—is seen. Suddenly there appears a gigantic, fiery banner: "The Spirit of the Pioneer."

Being a pioneer is almost a lost art. You don't hear people talk about pioneering anymore. You hear people talk about space being the last frontier and that there's nothing new to explore. But I believe there's a lot of pioneering potential in American business today. In fact I think one of the key things American business lacks is the pioneering spirit. Let me explain to you four benefits of the pioneering spirit, and maybe you'll begin to see how pioneering is another mark of a millionaire.

Pioneering puts a person on the front line of achievement. Every true hero is found on a front line. In a war there are two levels of command: primary command and secondary command. The primary command is in the field doing the job, dodging the bullets, and fighting for the objective. The secondary command center is usually back behind the lines—as far back as it can be and still maintain effective lines of communication. Most great battle decisions in the history of warfare have been made by a front-line commander, by somebody in the trenches. Front-liners are pioneers. You can be proud and feel tremendous about being on the front line of positive achievement with real people.

Let me apply this principle to business. Tom Peters has a book out called *Thriving on Excellence.* He tells a story of a company that hired him as a consultant. He visited all of their upper management people. He noticed that they hadn't been out on the streets for years and were out of touch with their workers and their product. Peters had heard rumors that this company had been producing a sub-par product. Its products were breaking down. So he did a sophisticated series of studies and analyses. Finally he put the research on the table and said, "Here's your problem. You need to do something about your product." These senior managers became irate. One stood up and looked at Peters squarely and said, "I don't believe this.

Get out of here. This is not our problem." Peters replied, "Alright." And he then walked out of the office, went down a hallway, got into a service elevator, went to the bottom floor, hailed a cab, and went to the factory in the Midwest where this company had its leading center of manufacturing. Peters interviewed the guys on the assembly line. He asked them if they had a problem with quality in that plant. They said, "We've been trying to tell management for years. We've got real problems."

Based on this experience, Peters wrote, "The people who count are the people on the front line. They know what's going on." And that's who you must be. You have to be on the front line of achievement. Do you realize that in IBM, a multi-billion-dollar giant, you can't even be promoted through the ranks unless you start as a salesman?

At Sears, the largest retailer in the whole world, you can't be advanced and promoted unless you have been on the line in a store, where it counts. In fact, Sears is an interesting story. In 1973, Sears was the predominant retailing company in the world. It led in every category of measurement. But then Sears was divided into five regional divisions. Their California Pacific Coast Division alone did more business and made more money than Coca-Cola did worldwide. This was a gigantic operation. But five years later, in 1978, Sears was at the point of financial collapse. They brought in consultants from everywhere to find out what was going wrong. All of them reported the exact same thing: "You've lost touch." "You must get out where the people are again." "There's no business like a people business. You know why? Because they're making more people all the time."

Pioneers are always on the front line. So the next time you say you'd like to throw your feet up on a desk in some corporate office, don't forget that you're on the front line of an exploding business, with people where it counts—you need to be a pioneer.

Pioneering keeps you on the cutting edge of growth. This is really important. As I have talked with hundreds of management consultants in the last two years, I find that they agree on just a few things. But they all agree that motivation is never automatic. Motivation has to be built and re-built all the time. It's never automatic. And so all these management consultants to IBM and Coca-Cola and Proctor & Gamble have books, tapes, and meetings. They believe that no motivation is automatic. It always has to be encouraged and supplied.

Now you hear some people say, "Well, I believe in self-motivation. I don't need to go to meetings or read books or listen to tapes." The problem is that those people rarely do motivate themselves. Motivation really starts with someone deciding to use some external technique to motivate himself. Many psychologists will tell you that a self-motivator is a person who exposes himself to all kinds of motivation systems and decides to take advantage of them. You don't just manufacture motivation from nowhere. You must feed on it. It's like having a computer with no software and you turn it on and wonder what's wrong with the computer. What's wrong is there is nothing in it. That's why when somebody tells you they believe in being self-motivated, look at them with a certain skepticism. Don't let people fool you with that. Everybody needs help in getting motivated and remotivated. So when it comes to systems of books, tapes, and rallies—you need to be a total believer in it.

I believe these external motivators accomplish several things:

1. They validate you. Everyone is constantly looking for a stamp of approval. I know you must learn to be strong and gutsy and build a dream, as we have explored in this book, and I'm behind you 1000 percent on that. But it's just natural for people to look for validation. And validation comes in three ways: through the written word, through respected authority figures, and through mass reinforcement—big groups of people giving each other support. Books, tapes, and rallies.

2. External motivators help overcome the "lag tendency." If you are not refueled regularly, you will lag. "Do you understand how life works?" Management studies show that whatever the business or program, no matter how much energy, enthusiasm, or motivation you pour into your program, it will always, inevitably lag after a few months. You can't stop it. The lag tendency is a natural force that comes out of fatigue. The recommendation that many consultants make to

management to help overcome the lag tendency is to come up with as many new wrinkles as possible to pump new life into their people. They're saying that people in good businesses ought to refuel constantly. I believe in this so completely that in the last few years I have gone into personal debt—10 million dollars—just to build facilities to supply motivation to people.

3. Finally, business psychologists agree that there is nothing more powerful in business than the charm of an attractive personality. That's one of the reasons you have books, tapes, and rallies—because people are taught how to be better people. They come out of these motivators refreshed, changed, and improved.

A pioneering spirit will teach you how to have a healthy drive for success. This may come as a great shock to you, but do you realize a lot of people view success as a negative and not a positive? They view the achievement of success as something negative. I really believe that we have to destroy that kind of thinking. It holds people back and reduces our productivity and creativity. We've got to overcome this philosophy. I'm talking here about developing a healthy drive for success.

A pioneer is a person who has achieved by his own effort and has earned self-respect. You must develop your own opportunities so that you can seize your future. You don't want to have to wait for a check from the government, and you don't want to depend on the kindness of others to help you financially. You want to be a pioneer, be successful, and be independent.

Last, I really believe in pioneering because it gives you the courage to operate outside the mainstream. There is deep danger in worrying too much about your respectability and status. Ron Ball has said on occasion, "Any business or company that begins to desire a greater show of respectability usually does so in direct proportion to its feelings of inferiority when it began; however, it was the daring pioneering instinct that gave that business its first success, and it abandons that dynamic spirit at its own risk." You see, the great pioneering spirit of enterprise allows you to operate outside the mainstream; that gives you more freedom and opportunity.

George Bernard Shaw had a great perspective on success. He said that there are only two kinds of men in the world. There are reasonable men and unreasonable men. The reasonable man is the man who doesn't ever rock the boat, the guy who doesn't want to cause any trouble and wants no controversy. But there is the unreasonable man who won't take it, who refuses to quit. Shaw further believed that all human progress depends on the unreasonable man.

Now, in some ways, the whole world looks at you and your efforts to succeed and says, "Aren't you a little unreasonable?" The pioneer is exactly that. The pioneer is one who is willing to challenge the traditional way of doing things. You must operate outside the mainstream at times in order to be successful.

In the early 1950s a man had an idea for a new business. He arranged it so that for a relatively low amount of money, others could buy into his business idea. He recruited people to do the business, and the enterprise was born. He worked and worked, and his new associates kept coming back to him and saying, "Hey, I'm having problems. My wife says I'm a fool to do this business." One man, after he had been in the business for about six months, said, "I went back to my old neighborhood in Minneapolis to one of my old neighbors and told him of my great new business opportunity." The neighbor laughed, made fun of this man, and said, "I don't want you here. I don't want your business here. If you bring this business into this area, it will desecrate our neighborhood."

Even so, these new business leaders stuck with it and pounded the streets and built their dream and advertised, and the business gradually grew. In the early 1960s a group of them got together to borrow some money for advertising. Every bank turned them down. One man said he went in to his banker where he had done business for years and asked for a loan. This business had been established for about six years and was doing well. But the banker said he wouldn't give two cents for the business. He considered it a cheap, fly-by-night operation that wouldn't be around another five years. And the man was refused the loan. Another banker wrote to the head of the company and said, "Why don't you disband your company and get into something respectable for a change?"

But in 1965 this fledgling company became a member of the New York Stock Exchange. It kept building and growing, and banks still wouldn't loan them the money they needed, but they still believed in their dream.

In 1985 they were listed as one of the best stocks in America.

In 1988, they were the 14-billion-dollar dominator of the fast food industry—McDonald's. Can you believe it?

Look at it this way. McDonald's was so successful outside the mainstream that it became the mainstream. That can be true of you. You just need to develop a pioneering spirit, one more important mark of a millionaire.

FOURTEEN
A MILLIONAIRE
BECOMES A PERSON OF
INTEGRITY

This whole book has been about the character traits and motivators that set successful people apart and make them distinctive. Now as I get into this last chapter, which concerns the question of inner character, I wish I could claim that all successful people have this quality—the honesty, values, and ethics that we call integrity.

Unfortunately I can't.

We all know too many people who have made money and have achieved some success in life who do not have integrity. Some people manage to get ahead by cheating, lying, and deceiving people. I would argue that such success is temporary and unsatisfying, but there is no question that some people out there who are making money are far from the model of integrity.

I can't tell you why these people have become successful, but I continue to believe that this issue of integrity is essential to a person of success. I believe that when you look at the great people in our century—Carnegie, Lincoln, Truman, Churchill, and many others—you see people of deep honesty and conviction. I believe that one of the marks of a millionaire is learning to be a person of integrity.

THE MEANING OF INTEGRITY

The word *integrity* suggests several things, but there are two parts of its definition that I especially like.

One part of the definition is contained in the word *incorruptibility.* This means that you are a person who adheres to a set of moral values and that you can't be lured away from them. I believe that people who are truly successful, on the inside as well as on the outside, are people who have moral convictions and stick to them. This is more important today than ever before. It is so easy to be swayed in your personal convictions by what is popular rather than by what is true.

I get worked up about the sin of abortion in this country and how it is covered by the media. We all know there is a media bias—that has been well-proven by many studies—but probably there is no issue on which the media has been more biased than the issue of abortion. One of the things that gets to me is the use of polls to determine what the public thinks about abortion. Frequently these polls show the majority to favor abortion. Now I have my questions about the validity of these polls, but my point here is that it seems as if the media's approach to the issue is not to determine what's right and wrong, but to take a vote. If the majority favors it, so they seem to be saying, then it should be legal. But since it's a moral issue, it doesn't matter if everyone in the country approves of it, *it's still wrong!* There's an old adage: "Wrong is wrong, even if everyone is doing it. Right is right, even though no one else does it." It takes a person of incorruptible conviction to stand up against the immoral and unethical practices in this country.

Another part of the definition of integrity is honesty. Being a person of integrity means being honest with yourself and others. It's interesting to me how many times in this book I have talked about making "friends with facts," being honest, facing the truth about yourself, and so on. That's because so much of success ultimately depends on being connected with the truth. Someone once said, "Only those on the level can climb the highest peaks."

THE VALUE OF VALUES
Have you noticed the popularity of the concept, "Be true to your values"? Have you heard that? It sounds good. It sounds like integrity. But let me

point out the deception of this concept. Everybody has values. Many values are different. Just because you value something and have a conviction about it does not make it *right*. Let me remind you that Hitler had values. He valued certain things like world domination. People who believe in abortion value being able to end human life at their own discretion. I think that's wrong but that's their value. People value lots of things, but that isn't a good enough foundation for a person of character and integrity. Your values have to be based on truth, on absolutes, on morals. You've got to move beyond values to morals—to godly morality—in order to be successful in an eternal sense.

DEVELOPING INTEGRITY

So how can you develop into a person of integrity, one whose values are not shifting with the tide of public opinion or arbitrarily based on personal choices, but one whose character is firmly rooted in truth and honesty? Well, this is a lifelong pursuit, and I can't hope to give you a complete answer in a few short pages, but let me offer a handful of suggestions:

1. *Do what is right because it's right.* It's interesting to me how many people do the right thing for the wrong reason. As long as the right thing fits into our plan for success and gets us where we want to be, then we do what's right. Well, here's a question for you: Is that integrity? I don't think so.

When the benefits to us change, then our convictions falter, and our values change, and our morality shifts That's not integrity.

I think integrity has a lot to do with our motivation for acting morally. It's not just a matter of doing right things. Someone has said that a true test of character is what we would do if we were alone and no one would ever possibly know or find out. So many of us act morally only because we're afraid of people finding out if we were to do otherwise. The Bible talks about the struggle of man being in God's image. God created us in his image, the Bible says, but that image has gotten tarnished through sin. The human struggle is that of becoming "conformed to his image." We can do the right thing, but in our heart still have the wrong motivations. We need to discover what is right and wrong—and I believe these can be learned through the Bible—and then we need to do the right thing for the right reason—because it conforms us—restores us—to God's image.

2. Take responsibility for yourself. I've said this earlier in other contexts, but the main idea here is that you will never be a person of integrity unless you realize that you're the only one who can control your situation. Don't wait for someone else to solve your problems. One of the bottom-line essentials of true success is you have to make a decision to grow up and not be a part of a "whining" generation. This is especially true if you are a part of the baby boom generation. As a baby boomer, you have probably grown up in a certain amount of affluence, and now you may expect to have the same affluence that your parents had. The problem isn't that you can't attain it, but that you may expect at the age of thirty what your parents finally attained at the age of fifty. You have to accept the fact that that won't happen. You can't whine about it. You have to decide that you're the one who will have to make it happen.You have to take responsibility.

I heard of a wealthy Christian man who was asked, "How do you account for your great success?" He said, "My great success came when I was twelve years old. I walked into my dad's office, and he said to me, 'Come over here.' My dad, a big burly guy, stood in the corner of his office. I walked over to him, and my dad said, 'Son, I've never said this straight out to you, but I'm going to say it now. I've tried to teach you, but I'm going to tell you right now. If you ever are going to amount to anything, it's not going to be because I gave it to you. It's going to be that you are deciding now to take responsibility for your own life. You will fail if you don't take responsibility. You will succeed if you do.' End of lesson. My dad walked out of the room." That man said that that was the most powerful lesson in his whole life. If you're going to develop integrity and character, you've got to take responsibility for your own life.

I remember when I had my stroke. I decided to fulfill a speaking commitment. The doctors didn't encourage me to go. They warned me there was risk involved, but I went anyway. I realized that I had to go because people were counting on me, depending on me to be there. I was responsible for my commitment to those men and women.

It's been said that for every benefit you receive, responsibility is owed. If you take responsibility for your commitments, it's going to release power into your business. If you are committed to take responsibility, it's going to do something powerful in your life.

3. *Always treat people with respect.* One night, I was going into a secured area where I own property. I had been looking at some houses and was driving back about two in the morning, and I stopped to get my security pass updated. There was a young guard standing there, and he wasn't all that polite. He said, "Who are you anyway?" So I did what I always hope people will do with me—I chose to treat him with respect. About five minutes later, the guy's boss drove up and said, "Mr. Yager, we're so glad you're here. Are you checking on your properties?" About this time the young guard started looking embarrassed.

I think that quite possibly twenty years from now, if by chance that guard and I meet again, he may remember me. I hope he will think, *Mr. Yager treated me with respect.*

There was an advertising slogan years ago: "People are our most important product." That's a brilliant advertising slogan, but it works just as much for you and me as it did for General Electric. It's true. Your success in life long after you're gone will depend far more on how you've dealt with people than on how much money you've made. Think about success in eternal terms. Remember the value of people.

4. *Never make a needless enemy.* The person who becomes your enemy today may be your Internal Revenue agent ten years from now.

Seriously, you don't know the future, and you don't know what that person is going to be or do down the road, so why make a needless enemy now?

Sometimes people become enemies through no fault of your own. In such cases, you can't help it, and you can't worry about it. The fire you kindle for your enemy often burns you more than him. But if you make an enemy through something you've done, seek that person out, and correct the problem. Not only will that gain for you that person's respect, but it makes you a person of integrity that will reward you in years to come.

5. *Be loyal.* The two greatest enemies of success are cockiness and greed. That's ironic because most people identify financial success with those characteristics. Remember the main character, played by Michael Douglas, in the movie *Wall Street*? But ultimately those traits lead you to follow your own interests at the expense of others. You begin to take advantage of people, and you become disloyal to the people you have business with.

What will happen is that when you need somebody, he won't be there. Loyalty cuts both ways. Life works by loyalty. You cannot have a good marriage without loyalty. You cannot have a strong country with loyalty—which is what patriotism is all about. And you cannot have a good business without loyalty.

I heard of a book that tells the inside story about how Washington, D.C., works. It examines the power structure, the government system, and the values and ethics of the nation's capital. This author says the most serious problem in our government right now is that there is such a cutthroat atmosphere. There is disloyalty everywhere. No one can count on anyone. This tends to paralyze everything, making it difficult for people in government to act with confidence.

A strong sense of loyalty is essential to the development of integrity in your life.

6. Guard your independence. Maybe it sounds strange for me to say this in connection with integrity. But independence protects integrity.

This can be taken in several ways. In my previous book, *A Millionaire's Common-Sense Approach to Wealth,* I wrote about the importance of going into business for yourself. Being your own boss is an important step in achieving personal success, not just for the opportunity it brings you to make more money, but also because of the things it does for you as a person. If you are independent in business, you will not be in a position of submitting to another person's, a boss's, instructions and sense of morality. You'll never be asked to do something unethical or immoral.

On a personal level, I believe it is important for you to be financially independent. That means getting out of debt and paying off people you owe in various ways. As long as you owe money to people—are dependent on them—it is difficult to be a person of integrity. You'll not always be able to carry out the convictions of your heart, but rather will need to fulfill the demands of your creditors. There is no freedom without financial freedom.

Ron Ball knows one of the most influential pastors in America. Not many people know his name. He is a "behind the scenes" pastor, but he works with thousands of pastors of every denomination. He is enormously influential. Ron was talking with him a while ago and asked him, "Why is it that so many pastors keep their mouths shut on so many key issues? Why don't they take a stand for the truth?" Ron's pastor-friend said, "You don't know? It's because they've become cowards. They're afraid of losing their job, their church, their parsonage." Ironically perhaps, many pastors are overly dependent upon their churches for their living, and consequently it squelches their integrity—the proclaiming of their convictions.

I believe God wants to set the ministers of America financially free. I believe God wants you to be financially independent. When you are free, you have dignity and integrity, and you can stand tall and straight and look anybody in the eye.

7. *Honor God, and God will honor you.* If you

know me, you know very well that I am a committed Christian. I make no apology for that. And I cannot write this book on character values, and especially this chapter on integrity without referring to the person who is the most influential person in my life—Jesus Christ. Now I know some readers do not want to hear me talk like this. It makes some people feel uncomfortable. If that's the case with you, I'm sorry, but I feel I need to talk about this briefly.

So I'll be very honest with you. If you are a committed Muslim and come to me and say, "I have a dream, and I want to build a business," I will help you. You don't have to be committed to Jesus Christ to build business success, and I certainly will not withhold my help and advice because you do not share my spiritual commitment. But I have to say that I believe with everything in me that the greatest reason for true success in life is the blessing of God, and I believe that comes through Jesus Christ. I say that as an offer, not as a threat or embarrassment. When you honor God, he will honor you. First Samuel 2:30 says, "I am the Lord. Whoever honors me, I will honor. And whoever does not honor me, I will not honor." I believe the most powerful statement on success in all the world is in Proverbs 3:5-6: "Trust in the Lord with all your heart. Don't lean on your own understanding. In all your ways acknowledge God and he will direct and lead your success."

That's the Yager family motto. Can you imagine acknowledging God and God Almighty directing your success? Nothing can be better than that. When you honor God, he will honor you. And I believe that honor does come through Jesus Christ.

OTHER BOOKS
BY
DEXTER AND BIRDIE YAGER

Don't Let Anybody Steal Your Dream
Dexter Yager with Doug Wead

This classic in the field of motivational writing has sold more than a million copies and is selling as well today as it did in 1978 when it was first published. Dexter Yager has influenced millions with his forthright honesty, compassion and desire to see others succeed. Here is a man who has "made it" in all the right ways, and who is willing to pour out the ideas that make for successful living.

BK10 English Paperback
IBK1 Spanish Paperback
IBK7 French Paperback
IBK16 Dutch Paperback
IBK21 German Paperback

The Secret of Living Is Giving
Birdie Yager with Gloria Wead

Birdie Yager, wife of one of America's most famous and powerful businessmen, talks about:
- Marriage: How to make it work.
- Attitude: The way to popularity and self-esteem.
- Your Husband: How to make him rich!
- Children: When to say no, and when to say yes.
- Health and Beauty: They are result of our decisions, and are not automatic.
- Money: When it is bad; when it can be wonderful.
- Faith in God: Why you must deal with your guilt and inferiority, or self-destruct.

BK96 English Paperback
IBK24 Spanish Paperback
IBK22 French Paperback
IBK25 German Paperback

Becoming Rich
Dexter Yager and Doug Wead

Inspirational and moving stories of some of the world's greatest people and the eleven principles behind their success. Includes Walt Disney, Albert Einstein, Martin Luther King, Andrew Carnegie, Adolph Ochs, Jackie Robinson, Thomas Edison, Helen Keller, Harry Truman, Coco Chanel, Winston Churchill, Arturo Toscanini, and Douglas MacArthur.
BK97 English Paperback

Millionaire Mentality
Dexter Yager with Doug Wead

At last! A book on financial responsibility by one of America's financial wizards, Dexter Yager! Dexter gives freely of his remarkable business acumen, teaching you how to take inventory and plan for financial independence.

Here is a common sense, down-to-earth book about investments, shopping, credit and car buying, and budgeting time and money.

Included are anecdotes about other successful American business people—to give you ideas about where to go from here!

If you are serious about financial planning, this is the book for you!
BK206 English Paperback

A Millionaire's Common-Sense Approach to Wealth
Dexter Yager with Ron Ball

Financial principles on which to build your life and your dream. Based on Dexter Yager's own life-tested success secrets, this book provides valuable instruction and direction for those who are just beginning to get a vision for success. Learn common misconceptions people have about money and materialism; Discover the eleven reasons to be rich (some may surprise you!); read about the five keys to financial prosperity—the dream principle, work principle, perseverance principle, investment principle, and people principle; break down the budget barriers in your own life; and learn common sense perspectives on managing money. This book will help you turn your life around.
BK315 English Paperback

The Business Handbook (1993 Revised Edition)
Dexter Yager with Doyle Yager

This is it: The most comprehensive how-to-do-it book ever offered for building your Amway business!

Unleash the proven success system with this easy-to-read guide which details the way to CHART YOUR OWN PATH toward achievement.

The Business Handbook, now featuring over 400 pages filled with strategies, illustrations, quotations and proven patterns, brings you the finest, proven techniques for **anyone**—from a new distributor to a seasoned veteran—who desires to build a larger, more profitable, highly motivated organization.

Best of all, *The Business Handbook* helps provide you with the latest growth-oriented, validated information.

Understand the historic relationships between direct selling, network marketing and interactive distribution.

Learn the distinct, powerful differences between our corporate sponsor's time-proven sales and marketing plan and other "just-like-Amway-only-better" would-be companies.

Prepare to tap into the phenomenon known as interactive distribution.

Develop yourself for future success by learning about:
- Winning
- Leadership
- Goalsetting
- Dreambuilding
- Loyalty
- Mentor Relationships
- Paradigms
- Trends in Distribution
- International Sponsoring
- Using the Latest Tools

Above all, discover the powerful pattern for success, empowerment and fulfillment used by hundreds of Amway Diamonds!

BK247 English Paperback

Successful Family Ties: Developing Right Relationships for Lasting Success
Ron Ball with Dexter Yager

Right relationships with the people around you are fundamental to your success in life—emotionally, spiritually, and even in your work. This book will give you high-performance, practical guidelines for dealing with the many important issues that may be holding you back from experiencing success in your family relationships. You'll learn to recognize the signs of trouble and to take steps toward overcoming:
- ruptured relationships
- busy signals in communication
- sexual temptation
- stress
- negative people

And with principles founded on God-given, timeless truths you'll discover lasting success in all your challenges and be sure to have successful family ties.
BK310 English Paperback

Mark of a Millionaire
Dexter Yager and Ron Ball

Character principles that will change your life. Develop the traits that are common to successful business people. From becoming a dreamer to being hard-working, from overcoming fears to seeking good counsel, from becoming a pioneer to establishing yourself as a person of integrity—these classic character principles are the foundation for success.
BK334 English Paperback

Everything I Know at the Top I Learned at the Bottom
Dexter Yager and Ron Ball

Personal stories and lessons from the life of Dexter Yager provide insights into the keys to success. Read about Dexter Yager's early boyhood experiences selling soda pop to construction workers; learn the important business principle he picked up from his early days selling cars. Out of these personal accounts from the life of a successful leader, you can learn valuable lessons for use in your career and your life.
BK351 English Paperback

Ordinary Men, Extraordinary Heroes
Dexter Yager and Ron Ball

Essential advice for winning the war for your family. Discover how the forces of our culture are trying to destroy your relationship with your wife and kids. Learn how to avoid infidelity. Discover the strategies for hugging your kids. Read seven ways you can win in the battle for your business.
BK380 English Paperback

Available from your distributor, local bookstore, or write to:

Internet Services Corporation
P.O. Box 412080
Charlotte, NC 28241-2080